From a Whisp

Barney Hoskyns was born in 1959 and started writing for *NME* after leaving Oxford in 1980. He has subsequently written for the *New Statesman* and *The Times,* and is a Contributing Editor at *Vogue.* He is the author of *Say It One Time for the Brokenhearted* (Fontana, 1987), *Imp of the Perverse* (Virgin, 1988), and *James Dean* (Bloomsbury, 1989).

From a Whisper to a Scream

*

The Great Voices of Popular Music

*

BARNEY HOSKYNS

Fontana
An Imprint of HarperCollins*Publishers*

The author gratefully acknowledges the following permissions:

'Hard Nose the Highway'
(Van Morrison)
© Warner Chappell Music Ltd
except territories Canada, Australasia, South East Asia and British Africa, for which
© 1974 WB Music Corp
All rights reserved. Used by permission

'Cyprus Avenue'
(Van Morrison)
© Warner Chappell Music Ltd
except territories Canada, Australasia, South East Asia and British Africa, for which
© 1971 WB Music Corp
All rights reserved. Used by permission

'Ballerina'
(Van Morrison)
© Warner Chappell Music Ltd
except territories Canada, Australasia, South East Asia and British Africa, for which
© 1971 WB Music Corp
All rights reserved. Used by permission

'I'm In a Low Down Groove'
(Roy Jodan)
© Warner Chappell Music Ltd
except territories Canada, Australasia, South East Asia and British Africa, for which
© 1966 Warner Bros. Music
All rights reserved. Used by permission

'A House Is Not a Home'
(Burt Bacharach and Hal David)
© Chappell Music Ltd
except Germany, Austria and Japan, for which © 1964 Diplomat Music Corp
All rights reserved. Used by permission

A FONTANA ORIGINAL
First published in Great Britain in 1991 by Fontana
an imprint of HarperCollins Publishers
77/85 Fulham Palace Road, Hammersmith, London W6 8JB

Copyright © Barney Hoskyns 1991
9 8 7 6 5 4 3 2 1
The Author asserts the moral right to be identified as the author of this work

Phototypeset by Input Typesetting Ltd, London
Printed and bound in Great Britain by HarperCollins Manufacturing, Glasgow

CONDITIONS OF SALE

For
Tors and Jake

'Music and mythology bring man face to face with potential objects of which only the shadows are actualized . . .'
CLAUDE LÉVI-STRAUSS

*

MRS DOYLE   I think voices are a true test of character, don't you?
ADAM WHITE   I'm not so sure. I heard a singer on the radio once, the most beautiful voice you ever heard. He wound up in Sing Sing.

From the film *Lonelyhearts* (1959)

CONTENTS

ACKNOWLEDGEMENTS

This book has been germinating in me for several years, and has come out of various articles written during that time: principally 'The Voice Squad' (*NME*, 12 January 1985), but also pieces on James Carr for *Wire*, Aaron Neville for the *Sunday Correspondent*, Eddie Hinton for *Soul Survivor*, Luther Vandross, Etta James, and Michael McDonald for *The Times*, and various sleevenotes for Charly Records. My thanks to Neil Spencer, Tony Stewart, Richard Cook, Cynthia Rose, Mick Brown, Richard Pack, Richard Williams, and Cliff White for their involvement in these pieces.

Thanks also to the following for guidance, inspiration, or just plain old favours: Steve Armitage, John Crace, Paul Drake, Alan Edwards, Tam Hoskyns, Andy Kershaw, Nick Kimberley, Biba Kopf, Muir Mackean, Peter McKernan, Bill Millar, Regine Moylett, Pete Nickols, Henry Pleasants, Christian Preston, Nicholas Rothwell, Edward St Aubyn, Will Self, and Mat Snow. Above all to my wife Victoria for her love and support.

For being part of my own vocal odyssey, thank you to Mark de Lane Lea, Paul Abberley, Jamie Hirons, John Sturton, Kevin Maltby, James Baring, Glen Keiles, Gregg Mackenzie, Nico and Maurine Mott, Helga Mott, Keith Patchel, Alex Ruhemann, Rayner Jesson, Maggie Ryder, and Chris Carr.

Finally, thanks to my agent Tony Peake and to Mike Fishwick and Richard Wheaton at Fontana, for making this one possible.

I Love You More Than Words Can Say

I begin this book with the conviction that few musical instruments are as 'moving' – whatever that precisely means – as the great voices of American popular music: Sinatra, Holiday, Cooke, Franklin and others explored in the following chapters. If there is a glaringly obvious bias towards black singers in my selection, it is because the singing which has most 'moved' me over the past fifteen years has been more or less rooted in the gospel and rhythm & blues traditions of black America; not because the book in any way concerns the history of 'soul' singing. It will, I hope, be a book about several matters: what makes one voice truly arresting where another is merely a proficient instrument; what is involved in the reception and 'consumption' of such voices; and – to a slight extent – what part the mythology of singers' lives plays in this consumption.

There are moments in recorded performances by, for example, Sinatra, Bobby Bland, and Van Morrison which literally produce feelings of ecstasy in me – just as certain lines in Edith Piaf's pathos-soaked swansong 'Je Ne Regrette Rien' 'tempt every nerve' in George Steiner, 'touch the bone with a cold burn and draw me after into God knows what infidelities to reason . . .' Music of course is plainly irrational, so beyond reason and articulation that it virtually beggars any attempt at writing about it. Indeed, George Steiner himself, in his *Real Presences*, tells us that attempts to verbalize music 'produce impotent metaphors' and quotes Hans Keller to the effect that all musicology and music criticism is 'phoney'. Thus I begin this book with an equal conviction of its possible futility: can I communicate anything worthwhile to you of my reactions to something so intensely beyond the reach of language? And yet isn't it this very subjectivity and this quality of being beyond language that I want to confront?

The Victorian Walter Pater said that all great art 'aspires to the condition of music': aspires, in other words, to a freedom from reference and representation, to a pure and transcendent medium of expression. A great vocal performance, whilst it is usually rooted in a lyric, and hence in the 'sense' of language, is something which has broken free of that language and taken off on a flight of pure, intoxicating sound. In the hands of a great singer, the most banal and trite lyric can sting with emotion. As Luther Vandross says, 'I can be coming out of a bridge and it feels so perfect that I could be singing about Rice Krispies for all I care . . .' What I want to get close to, then, is what Roland Barthes called the 'grain' of the voice, that absolutely unique quality in its sound which – for reasons completely closed off to reason – overwhelms me with a physical insistence, which immediately registers with me as if it were my own voice, my own desperate longing to cry out the pain and joy of this life. And in a profound sense these voices *are* my voices: they are particular vibrations and resonances which have struck deep chords with me, have become extensions of my own being and my own terrible need to ex-press. They are among the closer friends of a never-ending, occasionally almost solipsistic, dialogue with my self. For all I know, moreover, you will never hear my voices: how can I ever know what you hear when you listen to Bobby 'Blue' Bland?

Barthes raged at the way we say only 'what can be said' about music; what there is about it that makes us feel safe and whole as human subjects. He could not abide the notion that we merely match a singer's 'sadness' to our own comprehension of *what is sad*. Instead he nagged about 'the voluptuousness of sound-signifiers', 'something which is directly the cantor's body'. For him, furthermore, there were singers who 'translated' rather than embodied emotion, who only too happily complied with a received cultural understanding of that emotion. The great classical baritone Dietrich Fischer-Dieskau left him cold because he never 'exceeded' culture, because his every phrase was like a giant arrow indicating the appropriate emotion, whereas Charles Panzera, who sang before the advent of recording, did not belong to this culture at all; his art, 'swaying us to *jouissance*', communicated a paralinguistic truth which had nothing to do with Fischer-Dieskau's literary expressiveness. In Panzera, the body sang, not the mind.

The same is true of most of the voices considered in this book. Singers like Sinatra and Aretha Franklin create their own worlds and their own cultures: each of their recorded *oeuvres* constitutes an entirely individual relationship between sound and the shape of language, and a relationship which has nothing to do with sign-posting emotions. In great singers there is something instinctive, something almost innocent, as if at the end of the day their voices were really only ciphers for something altogether more powerful than the representation of what a song 'says'. The zoologist/anthropologist Gregory Bateson – concerned as he was with 'what important psychic information is in the art object quite apart from what it may 'represent' – liked to tell the story of Johann Sebastian Bach, who said 'I play the notes, but it is God who makes the music'. 'Not many of us can claim Bach's correctness of epistemology,' Bateson noted. 'The poets have known these things all through the ages, but the rest of us have gone astray into all sorts of false reification of the "self" and separations between the "self" and "experience".' No coincidence, then, that so much of the vocal art I want to write about comes out of the church, where there is no such separation, where the voice is the purest testament to God's love. Roland Barthes would have railed against the whole notion of 'soul' music, with its central assumption that the body is expressing some ineffable Other, but in fact the 'soul' is simply his 'grain' – the 'geno-song' exceeding the 'pheno-song', the body exceeding its culture.

How to structure this book? I have changed my mind several times, ever loath to group my voices into cultural categories: 'jazz singers', 'gospel singers', 'soul singers' and the like. In the end, though, some semblance of order must be imposed on them, and therefore I have decided to build each chapter around one or more of my particular passions, loosely associating these singers with culturally understood styles of vocal artistry. Thus Sinatra and Holiday are discussed in the loose context of 'jazz' singing; Sam Cooke is viewed alongside his gospel forefathers and his church-spawned contemporaries; and the mighty Etta James is seen as the original of a type of tough female soul artist. To an extent these are valid pigeonholes – if the voice itself can 'exceed' the socio-historical determinants of the prevailing culture the singer cannot – but really they are just conveniences. Although the cultural signifiers on a George Jones record (the

Nashville lyric, the pedal steel guitar) make it clear that I am not listening to a piece of jazz music, I do not necessarily experience his voice in a different way because he is a 'country singer'. Similarly, I do not listen to Winston Rodney *as* a reggae singer, but only as someone whose voice makes me tremble with awe and pleasure.

Each of my 'particular passions' is a springboard to discussion of other singers, lesser voices for the most part but all of them possessed of some ineradicable 'grain' that makes them special and different. Some, like Otis Redding and Marvin Gaye, are demoted from the pantheon of vocal deities to which they have hitherto been granted eternal membership. (Even Aretha Franklin and Van Morrison, 'particular passions' in Chapters VII and X respectively, come in for some overdue revisionist demystification.) Others are obscure names rescued from oblivion by fanatical devotees on the strength of two or three dusty old 45s. No attempt has been made to distinguish between 'major' and 'minor' artists.

My hope is that *From a Whisper to a Scream* will tempt someone to check out the voices of Esther Phillips and Little Willie John, Mitty Collier and McKinley Mitchell, George Jones and Winston Rodney; or just to listen in a new way to Frank Sinatra and Luther Vandross. The reader may not hear what I am hearing, but s/he might just find a voice whose cry answers the cry inside us all.

LONDON, APRIL 1990

I

Heartache on Tin Pan Alley

FRANKIE AND BILLIE

'Hey kids, dig the first takes,
Ain't that some interpretation!
When Sinatra sings against Nelson Riddle strings,
Then takes a vacation . . .'

VAN MORRISON

Frank Sinatra and Billie Holiday stand like twin colossi at the forefront of popular singing in the twentieth century. An Italian–American boy and a black American girl who did very different things with very different voices, they both transformed songs by the great 'Tin Pan Alley' writers into exquisite, definitive miniatures of loss and exhilaration, and every 'jazz' singer who has followed them has sung in the shadow they cast over their chosen art.

For contemporary pop culture, Frank Sinatra is either the balding Vegas hoodlum who crooned 'Strangers in the Night' and 'My Way' and still sells out the Albert Hall at £150 a ticket or he is the hipster icon of *The Man with the Golden Arm* and a singer of mythical genius. Until you start actively listening to his classic recordings, whether of the '40s or '50s, it is only too easy to take him for granted as one of the great *stars* of our time, a star as much on the plane of, say, Jackie Kennedy as on that of his fellow musical legends. I hadn't given him much thought one way or the other until Capitol began issuing their digitally remastered Sinatra LPs in the mid-'80s. I think the first one I listened to was *Where Are You?* (1957), an album recorded not with his most famous arranger, Nelson Riddle, but with Gordon Jenkins, whose lushly sentimental strings have come in for more than their fair share of abuse over the years. With the album cover in front of me, a typically, irresistibly melancholy painting of Sinatra looking abandoned and desolate, I played through the twelve songs, from the opening title track to the closing 'Baby, Won't You Please Come Home', and gave myself up to an experience of amazement and pleasure I shall never forget.

Subsequently I have discovered all kinds of minor details about the songs, each one a classic example of Tin Pan Alley craftsmanship. 'The Night We Called It A Day' had been cut by Sinatra back in 1942 when he was still with the Tommy Dorsey band; 'I'm a Fool to Want You', one of only a handful of songs he himself has played a part in writing, had first been recorded on an anguished night in March 1951, when both his career and his marriage to the actress Ava Gardner were in tatters. So this was a singer revisiting old haunts, performing with a kind of hindsight; 'I'm a Fool', indeed, had a passionate dignity about it that its tormented original crucially lacked. But what of the voice, consumed for the first time without any prejudicial information, that great deep croon which everyone in the Western world somehow *knows* without even thinking about it?

Sinatra's of all voices is one that lends dignity to loneliness, makes it not just bearable but positively romantic. To listen to the balladeering Sinatra on a Walkman is to lose oneself in a defiantly private universe of loss and regret. 'Can't you make the music eeeaasy and sad?' he asks in the classic 'One for My Baby', and it's the very correlation of ease and sadness (in the 1947 Columbia version it was '*pretty* and sad') which is so seductive. Keats knew that pleasure and joy are inextricably bound to melancholy; in the Sinatra of 'saloon' songs like 'One for My Baby' or 'Guess I'll Hang My Tears Out to Dry' it is clear that pleasure actually *derives* from melancholy – as Sinatra himself knows only too well every time he introduces his saloon medley with the following corny preface: 'We are now about to view a cat who's been living it up all by himself for some time . . . one morning he wakes, and he decides he's gonna go out among us and see if he can get back into the mainstream again; and he falls into a small saloon and proceeds to tell his story to the bartender.'

But why does this voice say so much more about loss and loneliness than all the other crooning, vaguely jazzy balladeers do? Probably because it is never showy or histrionic. Notes dilate, coil and uncoil within the superb legato phrasing, but always he holds back, breezes through, breaststrokes it. This is the leisureliness of the Italian *bel canto* tradition, but with an extra panache and gravity, what Arnold Shaw called his 'constant counter-point of toughness and tenderness'. Listen to the voice on Walkman and revel in its intimacy, its conversational ease, the little frayed notes at the end of sustained phrases. The control is awesome: when he holds a long note it seems almost to unfurl, changing shape as it opens out. John Rockwell in *Sinatra: An American Classic* points out, too, that the voice is defined by Sinatra's accent, 'a blend of his Hoboken–New York roots with broad aristocratic "a"s'. Gene Lees called his vowels 'almost Oxonian'. In fact, there is something of the actor in his enunciation – the music of language itself – though nothing that compromises the fundamental sincerity and vulnerability in his singing. Whatever the accent stems from, only Sinatra can imprint such exquisite shapes into words: who else ever sang 'matter' or 'parted' or 'gentle' like he does?

The young Sinatra of the Harry James and Tommy Dorsey bands, and of the solo Columbia years for the most part, lacks the rounded resonance, the huge power of the Capitol recordings. There is marvellous control here – a detached kind of grace – but the voice is closer to the light, loose-jointed crooning style pioneered by his first model Bing Crosby. As a scrawny, callow boy in a college bow-tie, his singing has what Jonathan Schwartz called a 'virginal caress' about it, a dreamy innocence that went hand in hand with the role he played for a generation of bobby-soxers pining for their GI sweethearts. Doubtless technical matters of microphones and recording had much to do with it, but on his '40s recordings – the original 'There's No You' is a good example – he frequently gets submerged under Alex Stordahl's orchestrations, sounding more like an airy tenor than the baritone he was. One notices an extra richness in the legato phrasing of 1952's 'Why Try to Change Me Now', recorded at the very end of his decline on Columbia, and by the time his first Capitol long-player, *Songs for Young Lovers*, was recorded a year later, the voice we know as Sinatra's today was finally in evidence. Pulling himself out of his post-heartthrob slump with a crucial role in *From Here to Eternity*, filmed in the spring of 1953, he consolidated his Oscar-winning triumph with this 10″ prototype concept album that included both 'My Funny Valentine' and 'I Get a Kick Out of You'.

As much as he is a consummate ballad singer, of course,

Sinatra is one of the masters of swing, as his effortlessly sassy 'Get a Kick' makes clear. This is the suave flipside of the broken-hearted balladeer, a lounge lizard whose every intonation is a tongue-in-cheek play on rhythm and rubato. Listen to the almost overdone articulation of 'roaring' and 'boom!' on 'Night and Day' or 'punch drunk' on 'I Wish I Were in Love Again' (both 1957). Listen to 'terrifffffically' on 'Get a Kick' or 'rrrrunning' on 'You Make Me Feel So Young'. And yet it's the down-trodden lover wandering the naked city under streetlights – the character bathed in lurid phosphorescent green on the cover of *In the Wee Small Hours of the Morning* (1955) – that means so much to people. What we live for are lines like 'Probably I'm boring you . . .' on 'What's New' and 'We'll go on living our own way of living . . .' on Gordon Jenkins's 'Good-Bye'. Or the whole of Alec Wilder's bare, haunted 'Where Do You Go?' on *No One Cares* (1959), where the great bell-like voice is more cavernous, more bleakly beautiful than ever. As Ella Fitzgerald said, 'it's always been just this little guy telling his story'. On up-tempo numbers, in contrast, the attitude of easy bravado is too set, too stylized.

Sinatra alone has survived the decline of the singing style he himself pioneered. After suffering one alarming slump at the end of the '40s, he made sure it never happened again. If his '60s and '70s were short on pop hits, he managed to turn himself into a star of such legendary proportions that it hardly mattered. He transcended time, if only by a willingness to experiment with all manner of trends and developments, from the sickly bossa nova of Antonio Carlos Jobim in 1967 to the work of a new generation of singer–songwriters (Jimmy Webb, Joni Mitchell, Neil Diamond, *et al*) in the '70s. True, depression and disillusion with the state of pop music at the end of the '60s prompted a premature 'retirement' in 1971, but three years later he was back as Ol' Blue Eyes, and by the end of the decade he was once again an undisputed superstar. The voice, too, which had had its sticky patches in the '60s, seemed in fine condition; Gary Giddins reported great form on a 1978 tour, while the following year's *Trilogy* went back to Sinatra's Tin Pan Alley roots with superb versions of songs like 'All of Me', 'Let's Face the Music', and 'More than You Know'. If things sounded a little strained by the time of *LA is My Lady* (1984), a reunion with *Sinatra at the Sands*-producer Quincy Jones, the essential timbre remained intact: 'Stormy Weather' was croaky, but the up-tempo material – 'Teach Me Tonight', 'Mack the Knife' – was brilliantly assured. Even his London Arena shows in July 1990 were redeemed by the rhythm and resonance in his singing. The timbre was cracked and the legato shot to pieces, but one could only applaud the bravery of his attempt at the Rodgers & Hart masterpiece 'My Heart Stood Still'.

Sinatra remains the great male exponent of a certain kind of song – the kind they don't write any more. Of the many fine singers who have come under his all-encompassing and inescapable influence – a list that would include such unhip but eminently worthy names as Tony Bennett, Jack Jones, Vic Damone, and Dick Haymes – none has come very close to touching him. Or escaping him, for that matter: Sinatra has made so many great songs his own that most sound as though they couldn't have been written for anyone else. I can't think of a better way to sum up my love for him than to say that, more than any other of its kind, his voice makes sense of sadness. And as such, it is one of the great instruments of redemption available to man.

It is a measure of Billie Holiday's greatness that Frank Sinatra, whose huge baritone couldn't have been further removed from the sound of her thin soprano, claimed her as his 'single greatest musical influence'. 'It has been a warm and wonderful influence and I am proud to acknowledge it,' he told *Ebony* in July 1958, recalling how he'd watched her on New York's 52nd Street in the '30s. 'Lady Day is unquestionably the most important influence on American popular singing in the last twenty years. With a few exceptions every major pop singer in the US during her generation has been touched in some way by her genius.'

It is to Sinatra's credit that he gave this tribute while Billie Holiday was still (just) alive, since it sounds so like the many things which have been said about her since her death. More than any of the other tragic divas of popular music, she seems to epitomize the doomed genius of singing, her voice itself – at least by the end – ringing with a kind of death rattle. As with Sinatra himself, getting past the myth to the sound can be tricky.

Nobody sounds like Billie Holiday, either in her prime or in her last, broken years. Ethel Waters bitched that she sang 'like her shoes were too tight', and she had a point. When you first hear it you can't quite believe that this is the voice of jazz legend: surely it must be bigger, you think, as if the 'size' of the voice should somehow be proportionate to its reputation. Holiday had no truck with this, although her sneering belied a profound insecurity about her own talent. 'What difference how big a tone is or how small,' she said of her dearest cohort Lester Young's playing, 'as long as his line was moving in that wonderful way . . . there ain't no rule saying everybody's got to deliver the same damn volume or tone.' She might easily have been speaking of her own playing, which often followed the same sleepy trajectories as Young's.

Holiday's earliest sides on Columbia, recorded six years after she trekked up to New York from her hometown Baltimore in the summer of 1927, are light and jaunty, the playful cooings of a blithe spirit 'havin' myself a time'. John Hammond paired her with pianist Teddy Wilson, and the resulting recordings – nearly a hundred of them over a period of seven years – are miracles of small-band swing featuring the cream of jazz players from the bands of Duke Ellington and Count Basie. Despite the fact that black singers only got songpluggers' leftovers in those days, Wilson and Holiday more than made the best of the twee material at their disposal. As Brian Case wrote in a beautiful *Time Out* piece in 1984, she 'recycled rubbish into roses', transmuting the work of hacks into vehicles of vocal bravura.

Everything is there on sides like 'If My Heart Could Only Talk' and 'Says My Heart' bar the bittersweet ambivalence of her maturity in the late '30s. Her timing is already completely instinctual, with phrases draped effortlessly across the four-square beat like strings of pearls. Her entries glide out of thin air, always one subtle step ahead of that beat. And she is enjoying the precision and physicality of words: listen to her lazy, labial 'l's in 'Falling in Love Again' or the delicacy in a maudlin trinket like 'Ghost Of Yesterday'. All that is missing is the schizoid sense one has in her later work of a voice that is equal parts lost child and tottering, tipsy crone: a Little Mother Time prematurely old with suffering.

In *Lady Sings the Blues* (1956), that slightly suspect autobiography she wrote with the help of William Duffy, Holiday says that, as a messed-up teenager starting out in Harlem clubs like Pod's and Jerry's, what she wanted more than anything was 'Bessie's big sound and Pops' [Louis Armstrong's] feeling'. As it turned out, she had little of either, and certainly not much of Bessie Smith's haughty, oratorical delivery. But something 'bigger', something which drags and moans and bleeds in the voice, comes through on her own 'Long Gone Blues', as well as on her readings of W. C. Handy's 'St Louis Blues' and 'Loveless

Love'. 'I been your slave ever since I been your babe', she aches
on 'Long Gone Blues', and one is immediately aware of a richer
legato with flattened blues notes. This is the prelude to those
songs which brought out her very best, yet which necessarily
induce pleasure of a rather ambivalent kind: 'All of Me', 'Soli-
tude', 'Am I Blue', 'Love Me Or Leave Me'. For what one
is hearing here is a forlorn apathy, an irresistible listlessness,
punctuated only by cries that betray the more frantic hurt inside.
This is Billie in her low-down groove, keeping emotion at arm's
length, simulating the diffidence and stoned remove of Lester
Young's sax. 'My heart has no sense of humour, dear/As far as
you're concerned', she sighs, but every vibrato phrase has a
ghostly whimsy about it.

Gene Lees observed that Holiday sang pop music in a jazz
context, and that she partook of the 'feeling' of jazz, 'a curiously
ambivalent joy–pain'. She herself knew of this ambivalence when
as a child she listened to Bessie and 'Pops' in a Baltimore whore-
house. Of Louis Armstrong's 'West End Blues' she said: 'The
meaning used to change, depending on how I felt. Sometimes
the record would make me so sad I'd cry up a storm. Other
times the same damn record would make me so happy I'd forget
about how much hard-earned money it was costing me to listen
to it.' Just as her most anguished torch songs have an oddly
triumphant air about them, so underpinning even the most win-
some of her love songs is an attitude of almost fatalistic resignation. More than most singers, Holiday knew that her art
transcended black-and-white notions of happy and sad; that
singing itself involved reaching for something beyond such
frames of reference. At times she became pure voice, a flow of
notes abandoned to the breeze of rhythm.

Things changed when New York's downtown art crowd took
her up as their own *chanteuse* in the late '30s and gave her a

residency at the Café Society. When she cut 'Strange Fruit', as brilliant a piece of polemic as it was, she made the uneasy transition to the status of Artist – one that she, like most street junkies, was never comfortable with – and came under the influence of cabaret singer Mabel Mercer. Mercer's emphasis on the lyrics of songs helped to change Billie from someone who worked as part of a jazz line-up to a singer who merely required accompaniment. When it came time to record songs like 'Lover Man' for Decca in the '40s, she asked Milt Gabler if she could try string arrangements for a change. The results were less than happy, especially since the voice was in any case deteriorating.

Holiday always denied that her voice, which never had much range at the best of times, was suffering. But then she never really admitted she had a drugs problem either. 'Anybody who knows anything about singing says I'm for sure singing better than I ever have in my life,' she protests rather unconvincingly in *Lady Sings the Blues*. 'If you don't think so, just listen to some of my old sides like "Lover Come Back" or "Yesterdays" and then listen to the same tunes as I have recorded them again in recent years. Listen and trust your own ears. For God's sake don't listen to the tired old columnists who are still writing about the good old days twenty years ago.'

In some ways her protests are valid, though it depends on your taste. By the late recordings for Verve in the '50s, the insouciant grace of her Columbia years has lost out to something harsh and tired, giving one the curious sensation that she is singing somehow on the *edge* of her voice, but that very quality exerts a certain fascination, and back in the musical surroundings which suited her best – small bands featuring sidemen such as Harry Edison and Benny Carter – she revisits the likes of 'God Bless the Child' and 'Love Me Or Leave Me' to devastating effect. This is the Billie whose hold on life feels pretty tenuous, who may have transcended self-pity but who is in some danger of drifting away from life altogether. And yet if the pleasure one can take in something like the Johnny Mercer song 'I Thought About You' – as old and cracked and defeated as she ever got – must be deemed suspect, even here, at the last gasp, when one can hear the phlegm of a death rattle in her throat, the intelligence in her phrasing is mercurial. And even here she does something therapeutic, slows the world down for a minute, gives one calm and a sense of what Simone Weil called 'holy indifference'.

'You never heard singing so slow, so lazy, with such a drawl,' the actor Ray Cooper had told Apollo-owner Frank Schiffmann back in the '30s. 'It ain't the blues, but I don't know what it is.' Thirty years after Billie Holiday's death are we any the wiser?

There are other tragic divas who have something of Holiday's effect on me, and in each of their voices there is a curious harshness, a knife edge of beauty that transfixes the ear as Ella Fitzgerald and Sarah Vaughan never could. What initially sounds melodramatic in Edith Piaf's declamations soon becomes mesmerizing: the piercing vibrato, the little ring in the roof of the mouth, a sound more regally sweeping than Billie's but still, like hers, half little girl and half stooped old lady. Dinah Washington, who worshipped both Billie Holiday and Bessie Smith, sang gospel and jazz and blues in a tart, acrid voice that combined Bessie's power with Billie's pinched delivery, while Esther Phillips, another junkie, took the Billie/Dinah influence to a pointed extreme. Washington was prone to chopping phrases off short or letting their last notes slide; that Phillips, originally the teenage prodigy 'Little' Esther, built a whole technique out of these and other quirks while still making beautiful noises, was remarkable. From her feisty early sides on Savoy through a '60s album of country songs and the live jazz set from 1970 *Burnin'*, all the

way to overlooked soul tracks like the brilliant 'Woman Enough'
(1981, three years before her death), Phillips managed to communicate a caustic version of Holiday's *ennui* with a voice that
strains and rages against its own restrictions. No long elegant
phrases here, just a weird timbre and an even weirder concept
of timing.

II

Pretty Boys and Church Wreckers

SAM COOKE, JACKIE WILSON, AND THE VOCAL GROUPS

Beautiful Screamers: the great gospel leads

It is a white cliché that the great black soul voices all came out of the church. Whites, critics and consumers alike, have so sentimentalized the idea of the black church that it has become, ironically, a secular myth divorced from any religious context. Yet few fans of 'classic' soul, be it Stax or the churchier side of Tamla Motown, actually make the effort to investigate its supposed roots, and this may have much to do with prejudice against religion. Occasionally one sees token references to the gospel forefathers who had such direct influences on our favourite Soul Men: Archie Brownlee on James Brown, Julius Cheeks on Wilson Pickett, Claude Jeter on Al Green are good examples. But there is little sense that the many reissued records by their respective groups (the Five Blind Boys of Mississippi, the Sensational Nightingales, the Swan Silvertones) could be listened to in the same way and with the same pleasure as the classic records of Brown, Pickett, or Green.

What is interesting about the great gospel voices is not so much how good many of them are, but more the status and role of those voices in the overall *schema* of gospel music. Gospel makes the human voice the be-all and end-all, a pure vehicle of testament, and often veers close to equating intensity, even volume, with passion. The story of the great male quartets, above all, is one that starts with smooth jubilee groups in the '20s and ends with Julius Cheeks shouting himself hoarse in the late '50s. In between you find the accounts of the legendary 'song battles', when quartet leads would compete against each other to see who could 'wreck the church' or 'dump the house' most effectively – in other words, to see who was the current heavyweight champ of the larynx. The more women carried out in states of swooning ecstasy – and some of them even died – the better the singer you were.

Listening to the '40s and '50s recordings by these groups, it is hard not to see much of their art as formularized, manipulative technique. Because the emphasis is so strongly on the vocal interrelationships – harmonies and cross-rhythms – within the groups, there is furthermore a kind of anonymity about the performances. Which is doubtless, in terms of religion, as it should be. 'It ain't the voice,' said powerhouse gospel mama Bessie Griffin. 'Sometimes the squeakiest voice can say what we want to hear.' Thus the song battles were in one sense more like contests between teams or gangs.

Yet it remains true that the great male leads of gospel (the women are considered in the chapter on 'Earth Mamas') did achieve something which, to this day, transcends both technique and group context. And to this day some of their recorded performances cut through the gospel *schema* and affect one deeply as something more than swooning, bravura technique. When Bobby Womack said that Archie Brownlee had 'a beautiful scream', he wasn't being merely oxymoronic; there *is* extraordinary beauty here.

If 'soul' singing began anywhere, it was with the pioneering hard leads of Alabaman jubilee groups like the Kings of Harmony and the Famous Blue Jay Singers in the late 1920s. Influenced by the unrecorded Foster Singers in Jefferson County, hotbed of quartet, singers like Carey Bradley in the Kings and Silas Steele in the Blue Jays began to incorporate the fiery delivery of Baptist preachers into the smooth harmonic base of jubilee. The older guard of jubilee crooners called these upstarts 'gospel men', and scorned their exhibitionist antics. As one venerable old veteran says in Kip Lornell's *Happy in the Service of the Lord* (1988), 'Some people just get up and go for a lot of Hallelujah.' The discrepancy between the old and new schools is exemplified by the styles of Charles Bridges and Silas Steele in the Famous Blue Jays. You can hear the stilted mannerisms of Bridges in two selections on the *Jubilee to Gospel* LP (JEMF), first in 1927 with his earlier group the Birmingham Jubilee Singers, then with the Blue Jays in 1950, some years after Silas Steele had left and joined the considerably harder Spirit of Memphis Quartet. Sam McCrary of the Fairfield Four, the principal vocal influence on that very gospel-conscious bluesman B. B. King, said that Steele was less subtle but more emotional than Bridges, who could 'spellbind you with a lot of conflicting harmony' but was never as popular as his sparring partner. Listening to Steele's dark, hungry baritone on the Spirit of Memphis' 'If Jesus Had to Pray' (c. 1949) or 'On Calvary' (c. 1950), where he takes off on a spellbinding *a cappella* vocal flight that feels almost impromptu, it's not hard to see why.

More renowned as an innovator and gospel forefather is R. H. 'Pops' Harris, a tenor who joined the significantly named Soul Stirrers in the late '30s and changed them from a jubilee group 'raised up on shape-note music' into the first truly influential 'hard' gospel quartet. Apart from simple formal departures from the jubilee norm – above all, using two lead singers and 'switch-leading' between them – Harris was the first 'gospel man' to introduce the sweet slurs and moans of blues singers into quartet, the first to experiment with what he called 'delayed time', and the first to employ falsetto. The birth of the soul voice could almost be located in the 1939 'vanity recording' of Thomas Dorsey's now standard 'Precious Lord', where, in between the group's flawless harmonies, you'll hear Harris weaving, climbing, crying, moaning – doing the things, that is, which every subsequent gospel and soul singer of any note has done. Heard fifty years on, it's not a desperately distinctive sound, this graceful, airily bluesy voice, but in its meandering play – a composite of influences as diverse as Blind Lemon Jefferson, the Ink Spots, and the singing cowboys he heard in his native Texas – it patents a way of vocal thinking that you can hear not just in Sam Cooke, his immediate successor in the Soul Stirrers, but in all the great soul tenors who followed in that golden boy's wake. Listen to him on 'This is My Prayer' (on Tony Heilbut's *Father and Sons* compilation), taking off after co-lead James Medlock's introduction, and marvel at the purity, the concentrated *fineness* of his sound; marvel, too, at the way he repeats the word 'early' three times, threading each one through with dazzling melisma (a passage of several notes sung to one syllable).

The Five Blind Boys of Mississippi underwent a similar, Harris-style metamorphosis after the Rev Percell Perkins joined them in the early '40s. It was Archie Brownlee, however, co-lead singer in the group, who took the innovations of Pops Harris one crucial step further: in his heart-stoppingly intense voice Harris's easy ache became a sensual, shattering scream. But Harris it was who set the pace, and who indeed took Brownlee under his wing when the Blind Boys moved to Chicago. Archie is still comparatively restrained on pre-Peacock sides like 'When God Dips His Pen of Love' (1948), and even 'I'm Going to Tell God' (1950) is only marginally less serene than Harris. By 'I Was Praying' (1952), however, he is running free, screaming and phrasing with the harsh beauty of an O. V. Wright. ('There's No Need to Cry' sounds exactly one of OV's sides on Back Beat, not surprising given that gospel and secular sides on Don Robey's Peacock/Duke/Back Beat labels often involved many of the same personnel.) Where Pops Harris played the elder statesman, the wise guru, Brownlee was a prodigal son, an abandoned Soul Man screaming raw sex in the name of the Lord.

Julius Cheeks went Brownlee one better: as he told Tony Heilbut, 'I cut the fool so bad old Archie started saying, "Don't nobody ever give me any trouble but June Cheeks . . . that's the *baddest* nigger on the road." ' In Cheeks the 'hooping and hollering' gospel man almost became a parody. His frayed, ragged baritone pushed volume needles into the red and wiped out audiences and congregations all over America. Yet even he began as an R. H. Harris disciple, as you can hear on the Nightingales' (not yet Sensational) 1951 'Vacant Room in Glory'. By the end of the '50s, after a string of Peacock hits that included the classic 'New Burying Ground', Cheeks was all but burnt out, his legacy left to the mercy of the Mighty Clouds of Joy's Joe Ligon in the gospel field and to wicked Wilson Pickett in the secular one.

The two other giants of quartet are the Dixie Hummingbirds'

Ira Tucker, who had a squall rather than a 'beautiful scream' and profoundly influenced the likes of Bobby 'Blue' Bland, and the Swan Silvertones' Claude Jeter, who went the opposite way to Brownlee and Cheeks in developing the sweet, falsetto side of Pops Harris's voice. Although by the time the Silvertones were recording for VeeJay in the mid-to-late '50s Jeter had reluctantly added a slight gurgled growl to his voice, his forte was still to slay people with sweetness and subtlety while the group's hard singers hollered around him. You don't have to look much further than a song like 'Keep My Heart' to work out where Al Green copped the major part of his style. In his non-falsetto range, moreover (as on 1953's 'Glory to His Name'), he sounded uncannily like a young Aaron Neville.

By 1950 there were hundreds of quartets throughout America, most of them impeccably choreographed and attired in the finest matching suits. A decade later, black America was bored with them, and attention switched to their female counterparts and to solo artists. In R&B's parallel universe, vocal groups of all kinds had thrived on quartet principles and would continue to do so throughout the following decade: from the Dominoes to the Dramatics, from streetcorner doo-woppers to Motown superstars, a hundred thousand black male singers could have identified with these words of Ben E. King: 'Your buddies, they were your *heart*. You could get so in tune it seemed you all had but one heart between you.' It wasn't any different for Ira Tucker, who sighed: 'Man, there was nothing like singing back then . . . it all went down so *easy*, everybody came together on a key. It was like you were floating.'

The greatest single figure to emerge from the last years of quartet singing was of course Sam Cooke.

'That Pretty Child': Sam Cooke

Sam Cooke (or Cook, as it was spelt when he sang with the Soul Stirrers) was the first gospel man with pop appeal, and hence, unsurprisingly, the first gospel star to cross completely over to secular pop music. With his youthful charm and svelte good looks he was a different breed of singer to the bald, blind, screaming testifiers who'd preceded him as quartet leads. 'He did it in a different way,' said one of the older Stirrers. 'He didn't want to be that deep, *pitiful* singer . . .'

Cooke's voice was as free and boyishly cocksure as his appearance. Where Archie Brownlee and June Cheeks operated through Baptist hysteria, screeching themselves senseless, the new young turk soared over their heads with a lilting, acrobatic grace. J. W. Alexander, the white-haired ex-Pilgrim Traveler who became his manager in 1956, told him: 'If they understand you, you can come up behind the screamers and always get the house.' An Ariel to R. H. Harris's Prospero, he took over the lead spot in the Stirrers when the older man tired of gospel's ever-loosening morals. (When Cooke was shot dead fourteen years later, it must have seemed to Pops like the most savage nemesis; other Soul Stirrers met similar deaths.)

Jerry Wexler, prone as he is to making sweeping statements, was not being so outrageous when he said Sam Cooke was 'the best singer who ever lived, no contest'. For sheer verve and control he has only Wexler's greatest protégée Aretha Franklin, who knew him almost as an older brother, for competition. R. H. Harris said Sam was a great *thinker*, 'creating without throwing the background off', and it is that quality of sheer intelligence which he shares with Lady Ree. But the 'grain' of the voice is exquisite in itself: a sweetly melodic timbre with just the right amount of coarseness in it. Otis Redding, Rod

Stewart, and Terence Trent d'Arby were all influenced by it, but none of them comes near the right ratio of rough to smooth, sandpaper to honey, and none of them could begin to compete with Cooke's daredevil assurance on the highwire of vocal play and melisma.

Cooke's technique never varies too widely; in one sense you're listening to the same performance every time. But what technique it is, with its wide nasal vowels, its quasi-yodelling melisma faultlessly dipping and bobbing like a swallow. J. W. Alexander insisted on good diction, so that every syllable is beautifully clear and rounded: 'will' is 'wheel', 'Lord' is 'Loud'. There is the downside of being identified with a trademark vocal signature – the immortal 'Woah-ooh-oh-oh-oh' he developed with Soul Stirrer S. R. Crain was mocked in his RCA years by his Italian *schlock*meister producers Hugo and Luigi – but it so epitomizes his style that one is obliged to forgive its over-regular appearance. Peter Guralnick observed that Sam could convey all by 'a flick of the eyebrow, the tiniest modulation of tone', and it is the little turns and shifts in the vocal lines that dazzle: he never shows off for the sake of it.

The first Soul Stirrers session to feature Sam as a lead, a version of 'Peace in the Valley' cut in March 1951, remains the first and last occasion on which he sounded at all tentative or insecure. The thin, boyish voice squeaks and cracks, its thunder stolen by the mighty baritone of Paul Foster. Recorded almost at the same time, however, are the far more assured 'Jesus Gave Me Water' and 'Until Jesus Calls Me Home', the latter a self-composed song which has to rank among Sam's most beautifully unaffected performances. There is a lot to be said for the unadorned, yodel-free style with which he was content at this early stage. Other sides, such as 'How Far Am I Canaan?', are too pedestrian as compositions to extract anything more than workmanlike outings from him; only on 1952's 'Someday, Somewhere', another Thomas Dorsey song, does Sam start taking risks, throwing up superb cries and tilting with almost arrogant control.

The up-tempo 'Come and Go to That Land' of 1953 is another leap forward, with Cooke, in mesmerizing command, taking vocal lines to completely unexpected places. On 'He'll Make a Way', a year later, he is essaying falsetto for the first time on record. But it is really only with the great session of February 1956, the end-result of six years' unremitting work on the road, that the genius of Sam Cooke reaches its dizzying heights. Too many of the earlier sides fall too complacently into what Tony Heilbut called a 'quasi-hillbilly' style of gospel, with only slower, moodier songs like 'Any Day Now' and 'One More River' marking significant departures: on these, as with Aretha Franklin, one sometimes feels that technique supersedes all else.

Cooke's 1956 masterpieces – 'Touch the Hem of His Garment', 'The Last Mile of the Way', 'Jesus Wash Away My Troubles', 'Pilgrim of Sorrow', and 'Were You There?' – remain unsurpassed as quartet performances. The first three were cut on the same day, the last may have been Sam's final gospel recording. 'Pilgrim', with its stark, haunting instrumentation and subdued moaning, is his greatest moment ever, with each word – beautiful words like 'glory' and 'consolation' – placed with magical precision in an overflow of ardent loneliness. 'Were You There?' sounds like a last, desperate testimony from someone who knew he was going over to the other side – the sinner's side – for good. 'Were you there when they pierced him in the side?', he all but growls with grief, sounding for once more like an Archie Brownlee than an R. H. Harris.

The Specialty pop sides are much of a muchness, all variations on the lighter gospel style of the Soul Stirrers' 'Wonderful', although 'I'll Come Running Back to You' (released by the label after the phenomenal success of 'You Send Me') boasts an unusually soft vocal, and 'That's All I Need to Know' includes one of his loveliest moments in the phrase 'Be there to *hold* my hand . . .' Most fans of R&B and soul known what happened when this greatest of gospel scions made the big crossover on RCA, and either try to ignore the syrupy big band instrumentation and vocal backings on these sides or don't listen at all. You only have to hear something as simple and bluesy as 'Sad Mood' (1960) to speculate as to how Sam might have fared on a label like Atlantic, who were indeed keen to sign him. But RCA had little knowledge of R&B, and packaged Sam Cooke for white Americans.

Thankfully even Hugo and Luigi couldn't ignore the new soul sound which was starting to make itself heard in the early '60s, and not everything Sam did in his last years sounds like big band country'n'western muzak. The 'party' songs – aside from the seminal 'Shake' – I can take or leave, but 'Nothing Can Change This Love' and 'Bring It On Home to Me' (with Lou Rawls's parallel lead serving almost as a prototype for all the male soul duos to come) both show Cooke reconnecting with his gospel roots, while 'Somebody Have Mercy' is almost raucously bluesy. Then again, even the classic 'Change Is Gonna Come' is blighted by horribly schmaltzy strings, giving a kind of 'Phil Spector on Tin Pan Alley' effect which almost succeeds in subverting all the hurt of the song. It has been left to the release of a raw, warts'n'all live album from 1963 to rehabilitate Sam as a genuine Soul Man. Tony Heilbut sees the album, recorded at a chitlin' circuit club in Florida, as 'a homage to June Cheeks . . . in the growls, preacher moans and ad libs you hear a father's style invigorated by his son's', and if it is not quite that – it's certainly nothing like James Brown's *Live at the Apollo* of the same year

– it *is* live and lowdown, sweaty and swaggering, and Sam is Cheeks-hoarse by the end of it.

Eighteen months later Cooke was at the Copacabana in New York, Uncle Tomming his way through standards like 'Frankie and Johnny'. Strange boy.

Sobbers and Doo-Woppers

If Sam Cooke's sweet rasp was the major influence on the gospel-infused soul singers of the '60s, the '50s were dominated nonetheless by a school of mannerists whose high, swooning tenors reached a culmination of sorts in the outlandish voice of Jackie Wilson. Like Cooke they came out of the church, but unlike him they 'crossed over' into vocal groups that remained true to the black precepts of gospel harmony: no sweet teen warblings of the 'You Send Me' kind here. Some such groups simply changed from gospel quartets into secular ones overnight: the Royal Sons became the Five Royales and James Brown's Gospel Starlighters became the Famous Flames.

The 'sobbing' style, first heard to any real effect in Clyde McPhatter's 1951 début with Billy Ward's group the Dominoes, had its antecedents in three principal tributaries. The first was gospel, in which McPhatter was schooled during his adolescent years with New Jersey's Mount Lebanon Singers; the second was the pellucid crooning style of pre-R&B secular quartets like the Ink Spots; and the last was the tenor vocal style of '40s jump-blues singers like Big Joe Turner, Jimmy Rushing, and Jimmy Witherspoon. Big Joe may seem to have been a million miles away from Bill Kenny of the Ink Spots, but Clyde McPhatter brought the two together in a freakishly high voice that mated unpredictable, cavalier rhythm to refined, almost operatic diction and timbre.

The arch proto-sobber was probably Roy Brown, whose plummy, exaggeratedly *bel canto* tone formed the core of Jackie Wilson's voice when the latter stepped into Clyde McPhatter's shoes in the Dominoes. Despite the usual apprenticeship in church, Brown began his secular career as a Bing Crosby worshipper, making considerable mileage out of the fact that he sounded white. 'I hadn't developed my shouting or crying style at that time,' he told John Broven, but even when he did develop the blacker timbre of his late '40s DeLuxe sides, he retained the phrasing of a white *bel canto* crooner: 'I' is 'aahh', 'know' is 'gnaw'. Presley idolized him, and later recorded a far more faithful version of his 'Good Rockin' Tonight' than that old blues shouter Wynonie Harris did.

The flipside of the operatic neo-gospel sob was the dreamy, meditative balladry of post-Ink Spots 'bird groups' like Sonny Til's Orioles and Jimmy Ricks's Ravens. These groups were the fathers of doo-wop in the same way that R. H. Harris was a father of modern quartet, and doo-wop was itself a mutant relation of quartet. (Even the Ink Spots, however pure and polished their harmonies, played a tenor voice against the 'talking bass' interjections of Hoppy Jones in the way many gospel quartets did.) Sonny Til, whose voice Greil Marcus rightly described as being 'so emotionally distant, so aurally crepuscular, that it did not sound like singing at all', is the missing link between Bill Kenny and Clyde McPhatter, and there is still something of his entranced, drifting tone in Dominoes sides like 'I Am With You' and 'Don't Leave Me This Way'.

For the most part, however, McPhatter was temperamentally closer to the blues shouters than to the bird groups. You only have to follow 'Don't Leave Me This Way' on Charly Records' Dominoes compilation with its title track 'Have Mercy Baby' to see the real Clyde at work in a dizzying display of up-tempo tricks – interjected exclamations and asides, glottal emphases, fluttering cries that could equally well be laughs, all delivered in an effortless, sexually ambiguous, wildly melismatic tenor-cum-falsetto. 'I felt more relaxed if I wasn't confined to the melody' is all Clyde had to say on the matter. Gary Giddins cringed at what he called 'the sentimentality at the core of much transitional R&B', but this is revolutionary singing, as dionysiac in spirit as anything thrown up in the name of 'rock'n'roll'. 'It all came together in Clyde,' said Ben E. King. 'He made a wide-open space.'

Slightly more suspect, to be sure, is the delirious threnody of 'The Bells', the ultimate in Sob: here a McPhatter crazed with grief shudders with hysterical, orgasmic cries for almost the entire duration of the track, creating a nadir in sub-operatic bathos rivalled only by the white Johnnie Ray, 'Nabob of Sob', on his 1951 hit 'Cry'. And yet this is only the sob taken to its logical conclusion, for the sense of emasculated melodrama is implicit in many of the recordings by these swoon-inducing practitioners of falsetto. Only when McPhatter left Billy Ward to form the Drifters in 1953 did he begin using his extraordinary voice to bluesier, less histrionic ends. By the time he'd been demobilized from the Air Force in 1956, moreover, his prodigal talent seemed to have been tamed. The mood of the quasi-gospel 'Without Love (There Is Nothing)' is utterly bereft but quite free of the perversely exultant hysteria that characterizes his Dominoes sides.

Clyde died a washed-up alcoholic in 1972, but not without the consolation of knowing how extensive his influence had been. 'There were guys like Jackie Wilson, Ben E. King, Bobby Hendricks, Dee Clark, Donnie Elbert, and Smokey Robinson that came to me and said they patterned themselves after me,' he told an interviewer, and to the list he might have added one-time labelmate Hank Ballard of the Midnighters. 'I fell in love with the man's voice,' said Jackie Wilson, who joined the Dominoes as second tenor behind McPhatter in 1952 and went on to become the only sobber to survive as a major soul star through the '60s. 'I toured with the group, and I watched Clyde and listened . . .'

Wilson, initially known in the Dominoes as 'Sonny' Wilson, took the sob that had begun with Roy Brown in the late '40s and developed through Clyde McPhatter to a new and delirious extreme. The range of the voice was slightly lower than Clyde's, but if anything the melisma was even more elastic and intoxicating. Indeed, for all the reverential tone of his subsequent remarks about McPhatter, Jackie sold himself to Billy Ward by claiming that he could sing Clyde off any stage. Certainly he trumped the McPhatter of 'The Bells' with his inconsolably tear-choked version of Louis Jordan's 'I'm Gonna Move to the Outskirts of Town' (1954), even if he failed to give the Dominoes anything like the number of hits his predecessor had given them. The control here is dazzling, as he blithely jumps octaves and glides through notes like a glistening, slippery eel. As with Roy Brown, the slight 'covering' in the voice makes it a less natural sound even than McPhatter's; next to someone like Little Willie John it is positively pretentious. Yet its magnificence is never just technical. Even when as a solo artist he tackled such crassly inappropriate material as 'Danny Boy', or the classical adaptations of 'Night', 'Alone at Last', and 'My Empty Arms', the voice vindicated everything, soaring like a bird over Nat Tarnopol's string-saturated production. And when, thank heaven, he was given a great, bluesy song like 'Doggin' Around' or 'A Woman, a Lover, a Friend' (both 1960), the results were peerless.

Gary Giddins grouched that Wilson was really a vaudeville man, singing on bended knee as though his ballads were 'minstrel arias', and one knows what he means. Listening to him smarming his way through medleys on the 1962 *Live at the Copa* album, you long for something a little blacker. Less of a showman but equally pseudo-operatic was Roy Hamilton, who took lessons in classical singing from one J. Martin Rolls while still a member of New Jersey's Searchlight Gospel Singers in the late '40s. Handsome Roy's particular forte was sobbing, heavily orchestrated versions of white show tunes like 'Ebb Tide', 'Unchained Melody', and most famously 'You'll Never Walk Alone', with all three of which he had huge hits and inspired Sinatra-style hysteria between 1953 and 1956. 'My style is fifty per cent gospel, thirty per cent popular, twenty per cent semi-classical,' said the self-effacing sex symbol, 'with a touch of R&B.' By the mid-'60s, having in decline borrowed some of the baritonal mannerisms of Brook Benton and Jerry Butler, he was veering close to Vegas-style MOR.

More rooted in the R&B tradition of jump blues were singers like Napoleon 'Nappy' Brown, who could flip from a McPhatteresque sob to a barking gospel baritone, sometimes (as on 'A Long Time') within the same song. On the classic '(The Night Time Is) The Right Time', covered by Ray Charles before Nappy could make a name with it, he anticipated the frantic testifying style of '60s soulmen by several years, sounding as mean as Etta James said he was. After harrowing sides like 'What's Come Over You, Baby' (1960) and 'I Have Had My Fun' (1961), the latter a reworking of 'Going Down Slow' with some blood-curdling falsetto shrieks, Brown spent most of the Soul decade in jail. His last Savoy single, 'Didn't You Know?', was pure church, anticipating his gospel sides for Jewel in the '70s, while an obscure 1969 album, *Thanks for Nothing* (Elephant V), showcased the unimpaired voice in a more contemporary blues-rock style. I saw him in the '80s at London's Dingwalls, his bald head concealed by a turban, blasting out the umpteenth version of 'The Right Time'.

Little Willie John was the greatest of the proto-soulmen. He should have been a sobber, but not for him the freakish pyrotechnics of Clyde McPhatter and Jackie Wilson. He lacked the 'beautiful' melismatic power of Billy Ward's protégés but made up for that with a voice which to this day sounds more wonderfully *human* than Clyde or Jackie ever did. It's a bizarrely magnetic sound, this sharp, slightly hoarse adolescent wail, with notes flattened at random and words chewed with delinquent disdain. He erupts out of the smooth flow of '50s melisma with a raw, frayed angst, at once doo-wop-shrill and jazz-weary, cynically young and sempiternally withered. (Apprenticeship in the big band of Paul Williams had much to do with his unique phrasing.) Play his swaggering King début 'All Around the World' next to the wondrously economical ache of 'I Need Your Love So Bad' and you have the two sides of this totally instinctive singer, who did as much with his gaps and pauses as he did with his cracked, uncertain notes. He never sounded better than on intimate, understated sides like 'Let Them Talk' and 'Person to Person', or jazzy blues ballads like 'Sufferin' with the Blues'. 'Willie John's songs were about knowin', *then* missin',' said James Brown, who knew him at King and later recorded a Little Willie John tribute album. 'Missin' makes me scream, but Willie John did not scream it. No. But you could hear it, and to me it was very loud.'

The 'group' sound meanwhile reached its apex in the various line-ups of the Drifters, formed by Clyde McPhatter in 1953 and led by him through such Sob staples as 'White Christmas' and 'The Bells of St Mary's' until he was drafted in 1954. Where so many '50s vocal groups – like the gospel quartets on which they were modelled – got lost in the overall homogeneity of the doo-wop style, forgoing the possibilities of individual stardom open to solo artists like Little Willie John, the Drifters outlasted them all by highlighting their lead voices, above all those of McPhatter and Ben E. King. The latter's comparatively gritty baritone was a distinct contrast to McPhatter's high sob, as it was to Clyde's immediate successors David Baughn and Johnnie Moore. Although King only sang on eleven Drifters sides, and although he could hardly be compared with, say, the Falcons' far more raucous Wilson Pickett, he brought a harder gospel edge to the group's sound, crying with a harsh abandon over that primal 'beat concerto' 'There Goes My Baby' (1959) and turning Pomus/Shuman baubles like 'This Magic Moment' and 'Save the Last Dance for Me' (both 1960) into pop classics. Future solo sides like the mighty 'It's All Over', together with his membership of the primarily southern-oriented Soul Clan, showed the direction in which he was headed.

Ultimately, as Bill Millar pointed out in *The Drifters* (1971), it was Atlantic's very highlighting of the Drifters' lead voices that led to the demise of the group sound. Millar's contention that the new breed of producers – Spector, Bacharach, *et al* – drowned the intricate harmonies of vocal groups under cascades of strings and female voices certainly holds true for the East Coast sound: gone were the halcyon days of Penguins and Flamingoes, Monotones and Silhouettes. When Jerry Wexler said that '*bel canto* has been our byword' at Atlantic, he was all but admitting that solo singers now came first. For Millar, moreover, Ben E. King's replacement Rudy Lewis was symptomatically 'mellow and inoffensive', a perfect channel for the 'Teen Pan Alley' conveyor-belt of songs from Broadway's Brill Building.

Actually, the tragic Lewis had a beautiful voice, close to King's in tone and timbre but if anything more assured and more satisfying. On 'On Broadway' (1963) he's a young turk, so vain and flip it's hard to pity him; on 'Up On the Roof' (1962), as innocent a Manhattan metaphor for getting high as you could conceive, he conjures a blissful sense of ease and escape out of the Goffin/King lyric, phrasing with the casual perfection of a Sam Cooke. (One wonders what he'd have sounded like on 'Under the Boardwalk', the song he was scheduled to record the morning after he overdosed and died in May 1964.)

But Millar's basic point still holds, for the age of the sobbers and the doo-woppers had drawn to a close, destined to be remembered and enshrined only by trainspotter-style collectors in the '70s and '80s. If the vocal group tradition survived in the Temps and the Miracles and the Impressions, it never again dominated the airwaves in such a ubiquitous way. And in the south, where much of the great gospel-fired soul music of the '60s was forged, you could count successful secular vocal groups on one hand.

III

Two Steps from the Blues

THE GOSPEL ACCORDING TO BOBBY 'BLUE' BLAND

Blues singers have rarely had beautiful or even particularly special voices. Where gospel encourages almost Herculean vocal feats of testifying, the archetypal twelve-bar blues form which came out of the rural South and travelled north to Chicago has centred much more around the relationship between gruff, untutored voices and the guitars that accompany them. In the classic records of Muddy Waters or Howlin' Wolf, the guitar is like a second voice, answering and commenting on the singers' barked, stentorian expostulations. As Robert Palmer wrote, 'The blues may have represented an attempt by rural blacks to accommodate the demands of guitar accompaniment within the free-flowing strains of their field cries and work songs.'

But there are blues voices that haunt and astonish. The first time I heard Robert Johnson, the mysterious Mississippi drifter whose guitar technique provided the most eloquent accompaniment the blues has ever known, I was chilled to the bone by a voice so starkly lonely, so playfully amoral, it seemed to have almost nothing to do with any music I had ever known. Fellow Delta bluesman Son House didn't like the voice, but its raw resonance, its unpredictable and sloppy arrogance, slowly sink in and clamp you like a vice. High-pitched joker screeches are offset by low-down dirty moans: the playful psycho-tease of 'ahoooo, bebbe, weer you stay last night?' – 'a distracted, comic determination', in Greil Marcus's words – followed by the eerie puzzling of 'I mistreated my baby, but I can't see no reason why'. Robert had mean things on his mind. Among other early exponents of the country blues, Charley Patton's fierce baritone still sounds out from the crackles and pops of his late '20s/early '30s recordings, though Howlin' Wolf, one of his many disciples, took his barking style to a more satisfyingly blood-curdling extreme. Blind Lemon Jefferson was never as unsettling a singer as Robert Johnson, but his slurring tenor, a rural mutation of the classic blues voice of Bessie Smith, combined (in Robert Palmer's words, again) 'sprightly phrasing with an ever-present hint of lonesome melancholy' in much the same way as Johnson's.

Of the later, more urbanized bluesmen, only a handful of legends – most outstandingly, the aforementioned Wolf – stand out as remarkable singers. Wolf was already snarling savagely on his first Memphis recordings for Sam Phillips in 1950, barking out brutal songs of sorrow in a guttural rasp which, by the time he was recording for Chess later in the decade, had become awesomely bestial. To listen to the raging singer of 'Evil' or 'Smokestack Lightning' is to hear a stupendous talent revelling in its superhuman power, a voice of frightening volume but also of very precise control and modulation: hear him concentrate everything at the front of the mouth in the 'eee' of 'evil', or check the falsetto howl of 'Smokestack Lightning'.

When Howlin' Wolf left Memphis for Chicago in late 1952, Sam Phillips of Sun was left with a crop of local, younger bluesmen who, in time, would become leading R&B artists: B. B. King, Junior Parker, Little Milton, and Bobby Bland. These were singers who had been influenced as much by the smoother Texas/West Coast blues sound of T-Bone Walker, Lowell Fulson, Charles Brown, and Amos Milburn as by the 'gutbucket' tradition of the Mississippi delta; singers, too, who trod a midway path between the country blues and the more gospel-oriented R&B of Roy Brown. Both BB and Bland, who have remained close friends and musical partners ever since their early Memphis days, grew up singing in the Baptist church, and gravitated more naturally towards the impassioned, sobbing style of a Roy Brown than to the hoarse shouting of the Chicago bluesmen. As much as Ray Charles, whose celebrated welding of R&B and gospel tends to get most of the credit for the blue-printing of 'soul', they began to move away from the twelve-bar blues form and to incorporate gospel styles and arrangements into their songs.

Bobby 'Blue' Bland is probably my all-time favourite singer, the possessor of a cavernously beautiful baritone which has made the gospel-infused 'blues ballad' all its own. Ray Charles may have been the greater innovator, and James Brown the more dynamic symbol, but Bland – who couldn't have been given a more inappropriate surname – is as much a prime mover of soul singing as Sam Cooke. If early blues sides like 'Lost Lover Blues' (1955) and 'Woke Up Screaming' (1956) showcase him belting in a hard but quite stylized way, punctuated by sudden, distraught falsetto shrieks, the mellower, more stoical timbre which came to the fore with the aid of Duke arranger Joe Scott was stylistically a synthesis not only of gospel and blues but of white crooning and country influences too. Two impulses seem to inhabit the new voice of 'Cry, Cry, Cry' (1960), 'I Pity the Fool' (1961), and the whole of the classic *Two Steps from the Blues* album which featured those hits: one gentle and bittersweet-sad, with its elegant, considered diction modelled on people like Perry Como; the other angrily eruptive, with the famous gargled squall borrowed from Ira Tucker and the Rev C. L. Franklin, father of Aretha. On most of his classic sides – from the definitive reading of T-Bone Walker's 'Stormy Monday' (1962) all the way through to the 1969 version of the standard 'Since I Fell for You' – he eases through the lyric with the care and control of a jazz singer, getting by on the sheer beauty of his hugely resonant tone; at key moments, however, he bursts and lets out the imploded squawk which has been his vocal signature now for thirty years. As he once said of 'Save Your Love for Me', 'I sing it pretty and then go into the preacher stuff . . .' Joe Scott gets much of the credit for nurturing the interplay of these two modes, not least from Bobby himself. 'Without him I would not have been the singer I am,' he told me in 1989. 'In fact, I would probably have gone home to Rosemark, Tennessee and given up as a professional singer.' (Something which Modern Records, who'd recorded him earlier, astonishingly suggested he do.) In a chapter on Bland in his 1966 study *Urban Blues*, Charles Keil reported the rumour that Bobby was entirely Joe Scott's creation, and it is significant that Scott had produced both gospel and R&B for Duke boss Don Robey. Peter Guralnick, like Keil before him, emphasized the extent to which Scott guided Bland through every phrase of every song they recorded together.

The two poles of Bland's style in his early '60s heyday would seem to be, on the one hand, such up-tempo, sanctified-style numbers as 'Turn On Your Lovelight' and 'Don't Cry No More', neither of them a million miles from the fervent gospel-blues of Ray Charles (a far less interesting singer, and something of a sacred cow to boot), and, on the other, the hushed, austere concentration of 'I'll Take Care of You' and 'Lead Me On', where Bobby's Baptist reverence coalesces beautifully with his balladeering 'classiness'. 'My favourites are "I'll Take Care of You" and "Lead Me On",' he said in 1969, 'because they've got more of a spiritual touch to them.' They were still his favourites when I spoke to him twenty years later.

Between these poles, if poles they be, lie the bulk of his classic recordings: 'Stormy Monday', 'I've Just Got to Forget You', 'Two Steps' itself, and the versions of Charlie Rich's 'Who Will the Next Fool Be?' and Big Joe Turner's 'Chains of Love'. Whether singing horn-blasted soul anthems like 'Ain't Nothing You Can Do' and 'That's the Way Love Is' or country-inflected ballads like 'Share Your Love with Me' and Billy Sherrill's 'Too Far Gone' (the latter featured on 1975's 'country' album *Get On Down with Bobby Bland*), Bobby takes songs over and fills them up with his vast power. As novelist James Bey put it in the '60s, his voice is 'the lion which lies down with the lamb'. If it is Bland's great fortune to have enjoyed the endless stream of brilliant songs published under the name Deadric Malone – Don Robey's vehicle for stealing the work of impoverished tunesmiths – then he has made these songs all but impossible to cover, so definitive is the master's touch with which he has stamped them. As much as Sinatra or Aretha, he is a singers' singer.

By the end of the '60s, when he parted company with Joe Scott, the Bland larynx had taken on the slightly frayed, *gravelized* quality that defines it to this day. The secret is that it has only the faintest crack in it; because its owner has never misused or abused it, it never splits too coarsely. Listen to the sound as it fills out the whole skull on 'Chains of Love' (1969) or 1973's

'This Time I'm Gone for Good': there is nothing else in blues or soul quite like the dignified, withering resignation of this 'grain'. As Gary Giddins wrote, 'He is a screamer without being a shouter . . . always in control and never crackling into a desperate B. B. King yell.' One need only compare BB and Bobby as they spar and swap lines on the two live albums they cut together in the '70s to realize that where Bland commands, BB merely growls. The same goes for Little Milton, whose fruity baritone is a pure synthesis of BB and Bobby. It is significant that Bland, unlike BB or Milton, has never played the guitar.

That Bland still has his pipes in working order is a fact for which anyone present at his show at London's Hammersmith Odeon in 1989 would surely vouch. Following on the heels of the cheerfully pugnacious Johnnie Taylor, his slightly glazed, tottering appearance belied a serene majesty, and within a few numbers – a medley of 'That's the Way Love Is', 'Ain't Nothing You Can Do', and his first blues hit 'Further Up the Road' – the audience was rapt. If he held himself back, chewing diffidently through consonants and flinching away from the mike, when he let the voice sail it sounded more richly resonant than ever. Compared to Taylor's, his 'working' of the audience was a cool, even distanced affair, but then this was a different level of communication altogether. (Arnold Shaw noted that Bobby's appeal was his 'combination of helplessness and self-assurance'.) When he wound up the set with 'I'll Take Care of You' and 'Stormy Monday', the band (including Wayne Bennett, his legendary guitarist from the Duke days) barely whispering behind him, it was clear that the years had really taken no toll at all.

Bobby's post-Duke career – the label was sold to ABC in 1973 and he went as part of the package – has been a patchy affair. Gary Giddins captured all the pitfalls of the ABC period in his fine essay 'Bobby "Blue" Bland Meets the White Folks':

as with B. B. King, the label attempted – and not without some success – to turn Bobby into a product which would appeal to hip rock fans. The resulting albums, *His California Album*, *Dreamer*, and the like, were recorded in LA and for the most part consist of hokey, ersatz blues-soul outings like 'Yolanda' and 'Ain't No Love in the Heart of the City' (later covered by HM band Whitesnake). The country album, predictably, was slammed by critics, despite being a lot closer to his southern roots and despite producing one of his very greatest perform- ances in 'Too Far Gone', previously a hit for Tammy Wynette. (The imagination falters at the possibilities of the album he was once rumoured to be cutting with Tammy's ex-hubbie George Jones.) This is Bobby at his resplendent best, building from an airy baritone whisper to an aching howl, sailing by with effort- less grace, barely dipping down to touch the consonants in each exquisitely launched phrase. 'Gravelly *gravitas*', my friend Muir Mackean calls it, and nothing could better sum up the effect of these three miraculous minutes.

The live albums with BB notwithstanding – they're fun but hardly inspirational – there is little of lasting value in the remain- der of Bland's recorded *oeuvre*. In the mid-'80s, after some truly dismal records on MCA (who'd swallowed up ABC in the same way ABC had swallowed up Duke), he found a retirement home of sorts in Malaco of Jackson, Mississippi, since when he's made a handful of pleasant if fundamentally undemanding records. 'Members Only' (1985) was a good song, but the company, run by two white southerners who grew up listening to Bobby's Duke sides, hasn't come up with anything to match it since.

Bobby Bland's legacy can be detected in a legion of singers: in bluesmen who sound soulfully churchy, in soulmen with a leaning towards the blues. Four of the best are (or were) Geater Davis, McKinley Mitchell, Mighty Sam, and Z. Z. Hill, all of them, to differing degrees, straddling the boundaries between blues and gospel-based soul music. Vernon 'Geater' Davis, in particular, sang in a scorched, desolate, Bland-haunted baritone that put me in an unholy trance the first time I heard his shattering version of the Impressions' 'For Your Precious Love' on a John Peel show at the tender age of fifteen. Nobody knows much about Geater, other than that he was born in a tiny Texan town called Conroe and drifted dissolutely round the South in a vaguely Robert Johnson-esque manner. Somehow that seems quite fitting, since what one hears on chilling sides like 'Sad Shade of Blue', 'You Made Your Bed Hard', or 'Best of Luck to You' is an almost elemental loneliness, a Bobby Bland stripped of the veneer of sophisticated balladry and reduced to a primal backwoods groan: a 'beautiful groan', if you like. The throat is burnt, blasted by grief, and the phrasing sounds so weary and wounded you feel Geater can barely open his mouth. In the early '80s, shortly before his death, he cut a version of Bland's 'I'll Take Care of You' for James Bennett's tiny MT label, and an LP, *Better Days*, in which a very Bland-influenced squall made several belated appearances. Sadly, he didn't live to see his hero record 'Sweet Woman's Love' – a minor R&B hit for Geater in 1970 – on the Malaco *Members Only* album.

McKinley Mitchell was another extraordinary singer who ended his life recording for the shoestring clutch of labels run by James Bennett in Jackson, Mississippi. As an uptown soulman in '60s Chicago, he sounded like a harsher Ben E. King, quoting from King's classic vocal on the Drifters' 'There Goes My Baby' in his 1962 hit 'The Town I Live In', but by the '70s the voice had softened and deepened, as one can hear on the revisited version of the latter song on 1978's Chimneyville album *McKinley Mitchell*. On this and the similarly spine-chilling ballads 'Same Old Dream' and 'End of the Rainbow', McKinley does what Bobby

Bland does, albeit in a rather more idiosyncratic manner: that is, begins in a mellow, almost country-nasal voice, only to finish the songs in a torrent of squalled screams. (Of all the 'beautiful screams' produced by blues-soulmen, this is one of the most freakish.) Fusing gospel-blues tenor abandon with the baritonal vibrato of a Brook Benton and the eccentric nasality of a country singer, Mitchell, who died in January 1986, remains one of the more bizarre voices of soul.

The Bland squall found yet another home in the larynx of Louisiana-born 'Mighty' Sam McClain, a southern soulman whose Muscle Shoals-recorded sides on Amy include some of the best 'country soul' of the '60s: Dan Penn/Spooner Oldham ballads like 'In the Same Old Way', a tempestuous reading of Don Gibson's country staple 'Sweet Dreams'. When I stumbled on Sam singing in a tiny New Orleans bar called Benny's in late 1985, the highlights of his set were devoutly faithful versions of 'Stormy Monday' and 'This Time I'm Gone for Good', both delivered in a voice boiling over with injured pride. If anything, as with Bland himself, the voice sounded bigger and better than ever, the baritone deep and rich and the squall a cauldron of frantic, frothing anger. The following year, as chance would have it, Sam found himself playing Tokyo, land of the rising deep soul freak, backed on guitar by none other than Wayne Bennett.

Sounding more like Ray Charles than Bobby Bland, the late Arzel 'ZZ' Hill was an archetypal blues-soul growler and the man whose nostalgic 'Down Home Blues' helped to make Malaco Records the pre-eminent black music independent of the '80s. Malaco capitalized on that record's totally unexpected success by presenting ZZ thereafter as a Blues Man, which was disingenuous, if understandable: in fact, the Texan-born baritone had been more of a Soul Man for the greater part of his career, from raunchy horn-blasted Kent sides in the '60s to sumptuously orchestrated cheating ballads on Columbia in the '70s. And nowhere does his gruff, cuddly, teddy-bear voice sound better than on soul ballads like the Lamont Dozier-produced 'That Ain't the Way You Make Love' or Frederick Knight's 'This Time They Told the Truth': ZZ growling against a wash of sweet strings and female voices is somehow more satisfying than ZZ growling out a bland blues song. ('This Time' contains one of the all-time great moments of soul, when in the second verse the voice cracks on the word 'misery'.) Granted, there was one magnificent blues-based side in 'Don't Make Me Pay for His Mistakes', a sizeable R&B hit in 1972, but it remains the exception rather than the rule. ZZ had his own trademark version of the Bobby Bland squall, though it was more of a 'bark's worse than his bite' roar of defiance than a guttural implosion of emotion. Like most Texan R&B singers of the '60s, he came heavily under Bland's influence, and later recorded a version of 'Ain't Nothing You Can Do' for United Artists.

Just as Geater Davis died before he could hear Bobby Bland singing one of his songs, so ZZ died before he could see his own success make it possible for Malaco to rescue the greatest blues-soulman of them all in the '80s: without 'Down Home Blues' there would have been no 'Members Only'. At the time of writing, Bland keeps on trucking, seemingly determined to outlive his many disciples and imitators on that endless road of one-horse towns and one-night stands, and forever taking two crucial steps away from the blues.

IV

Earth Mamas

ETTA JAMES AND THE BELTERS

The earth mama is one of the great stereotypes of black American music in the twentieth century: I use it merely as a convenient umbrella term for a line of female singers that came simultaneously out of the church and the 'classic blues' school in the 1920s, a line typified as much by gospel matriarchs like Mahalia Jackson and Marion Williams as by lusty R&B singers like LaVern Baker and Big Maybelle. The earth mama is generally a big – busty or statuesque – woman with a big, belting contralto voice, and her business generally involves 'tearing up' clubs or churches and reducing their audiences or congregations to an emotional pulp. Aretha Franklin may soar into the stratosphere and shake up the firmament, but the earth mama takes you down to the greasy river of life and baptizes you in all its trials and tribulations. As Etta James, greatest of all the mamas and possessor of a powerhouse voice which has sung rock'n'roll, deep soul, funk, and gospel, put it: 'I can't sing how it feels to be on the moon, I ain't never been there. All I know about is how it feels to wallow in this mud, how it feels to be so greasy you feel like you just came out of a garbage can. That's what I got to talk about.'

Mahalia Jackson may have been telling us to 'Move On Up a Little Higher', but thanks to Bessie Smith she knew what it meant to wallow. 'Bessie was my favourite, but I never let people know I listened to her,' she said. 'Mamie Smith had a prettier voice, but Bessie's had more soul in it. She dug right down and kept it in you – her music haunted you even when she stopped singing.' Mahalia's Chicago mentor Willie Mae Ford Smith, too, had come under Bessie's spell, and more than any of the other early gospel mothers was responsible for bringing flattened and slurred blues notes into the gospel voice as we know it today. Her 'If You Just Keep Still' became one of Mahalia's greatest gospel-blues numbers, while her other protégées included Windy City legend Myrtle Scott and the 'Midwest Thunderbolt' Brother Joe May.

It's amusing to reflect that long before male gospel leads switched to the secular field and became high-earning soul super-stars, the matriarchs of the Baptist and Sanctified churches – Mahalia, Clara Ward, Sister Rosetta Tharpe and others – were displaying a far shrewder business sense than their counterparts in the quartets. Indeed, when the heyday of those male quartets came to an end it was the female groups – the Ward Singers, the Davis Sisters, the Caravans, the Gospel Harmonettes – who took over, producing in the process a stream of huge-voiced earth mamas that included Marion Williams, Albertina Walker, Bessie Griffin, Dorothy Love Coates, and Inez Andrews.

If Mahalia and Clara – Aretha's great mentor – had by the mid-'50s sold out fairly shamelessly in pursuit of the white market, the likes of Williams (who led the Ward Singers on classic sides like 'Surely God Is Able') and Griffin (who sang with the Caravans) remained true to what they saw as their vocation. Tony Heilbut described Williams as 'simply the most lyrical and imaginative singer gospel has produced', a purveyor of 'seraphic funk', and Little Richard acknowledged her as 'the lady who gave me my *whoo!*' Her greatest success came in the early '60s with the Broadway play *Black Nativity*, based on an album of Christmas hymns she had recorded. As for Bessie Griffin, anyone who wishes to hear a prototype soul perform-ance of truly electrifying intensity need only be directed to her 1950 version of Alex Bradford's 'Too Close to Heaven', recorded live at Memphis's Mason's Temple to the mass accompaniment of shouts, swoons, and ecstatic chuckles. Here you will find everything you need to know about tension and release, about coming out of a squalled scream into a playful cooing, about building an audience up to fever pitch and then dropping them into a heart-stopping void.

As with the 'beautiful screamers' who dominated the male quartets, there remains a sense in which these mighty church mothers are less interesting as singers *per se* than as channels of technique in the service of testament. It is rare amidst all the huffing and puffing and hollering that something personal, a genuine vocal 'grain', cuts through. Again, that is not the busi-ness of these voices which entreat us away from the private and the solitary and exhort us to melt into a communal rapture. Perhaps, blue notes and all, it is in the nature of this singing that the earth mama should almost be anonymous. The differ-ence between Bessie Griffin singing 'Too Close' and Etta James singing 'I'd Rather Go Blind' is the difference between redeemed and fallen man: Bessie sings towards higher ends, Etta sings within the sickness of jealousy and loss. As mother Mahalia said, 'Somebody singing blues is crying out of a pit . . . I'm singing out of the joy of my salvation.'

The same kind of anonymity, or at least interchangeability, might be said to characterize the earth mamas of late '40s/early '50s rhythm'n'blues. Like the original blues matriarch Bessie Smith, these imperiously haughty women, with their throaty indignation and endless challenges to 'Daddy', are always too much the knowing entertainer to be truly stirring singers. Over the cardboard-box beat, the tipsy trickle of piano notes, and those ubiquitous, lazily pawing saxophones, they shout the blues in a style which sounds timebound and anachronistic today. Of the voices which transcend the boozy context of their early '50s setting, Ruth Brown's was thinner than that of LaVern Baker, her principal rival at Atlantic, but possessed of a spunky hoarseness, a little catch in the throat, that made it more pleasing and more soulful. If her timing and wide, exaggeratedly mannered phrasing seemed to come from Joe Turner, the ultimate blues shouter, the falsetto squeaks she often used to finish phrases could have been modelled on Clyde McPhatter. Little Esther (later Phillips) was another oddball, an R&B Lolita playing earth mama in a precocious voice that sounded almost speeded-up, like a cartoon version of Billie Holiday or of her idol Dinah Washington.

Big Maybelle was earth-mama big in no uncertain terms, but her voice too went beyond mere hell-hath-no-fury playfulness. Even on OKeh jump-blues sides like 'My Country Man' and 'Jimmy Mule' (both 1953) there was something darkly nasal, a suggestion of suppressed gospel emotion that set her apart from the swagger of LaVern Baker and Marie Adams and Varetta Dillard. As much as Dinah Washington herself, a far less pigeon-holable singer but one equally steeped in the church, Maybelle anticipated the agony of the deep soul ballad, and indeed survived through to the '60s to cut soul sides like the astonishing 'Don't Pass Me By'. Tony Cummings observed that her style was neither jazz-blues of the Bessie Smith kind, nor the Kansas City style of Joe Turner and company; nor indeed had it very much to do with Billie Holiday: 'It seemed to consist,' he continued, 'rather of singing blues (and later ballads) in a voice totally cracked and broken with emotion, apparently unable to sustain any feeling other than world-weary desperation.'

Big Maybelle bridged the gap between LaVern Baker and Etta James. Like both Maybelle and Esther Phillips, Etta grappled with years of miserable drug addiction and sang with the acrid snarl of the born outsider. (As a buxom teenage glamourpuss with drugstore-peroxide blonde hair and a lewd 1955 rock'n'roll hit called 'Roll with Me, Henry', Etta had a brief encounter with her idol Billie Holiday that she will never forget: escorted into a radio station because her feet were so swollen she couldn't walk, the forty-year-old singer and junkie *chanteuse* turned to her young admirer and muttered the fatefully ironic words: 'Don't ever let this happen to you.') In Etta James, the earth mama – or at least, a streetwise seventeen-year-old edition of that archetype – grows up to be a veritable empress of soul.

From the off, she sang with the sassy gusto of a Ruth Brown – there are shades of Etta in Ruth's 1955 side 'I Can See Everybody's Baby' – but reinforced it with a gospel fire acquired in LA's St Paul's Baptist Church and a raging hurt acquired through years of childhood neglect. Like Faye Adams on 'Shake a Hand', a seminal 1953 recording which Peter Guralnick said 'might as well have been recorded in church', Etta introduced something almost masculine into the earth mama larynx, an intemperate wail that you can hear as far back as 'Roll with Me, Henry' – it's right there in her vicious pronunciation of 'Hinreh' – and that makes her status as Queen of the Earth Mamas amusingly paradoxical. (In her way, she's been as much an icon of butch female sexuality as Dusty Springfield: Etta's version of

Alice Cooper's 'Only Women Bleed' could be a gay classic.) It's this rage in her voice, one that informs everything from her '50s jump-rock'n'roll hits through the jazzy blues ballads and gospel-drenched soul of the '60s to the funk of the '70s, which makes it such a cathartic instrument. It's not exactly subtle or supple, this belting great contralto: it doesn't go in for much melisma or high-wire virtuosity, and couldn't compete with many of the gospel matriarchs. But the huge resonance of its hurt is like a primal field holler, an awesome wail dredged from the bowels of her being, and she need only let out a single sustained note to pierce you clean through.

Etta's golden period came after she washed up in a Chicago fleapit in 1960 and signed to Chess subsidiary Argo. A string of rather twee ballads – 'All I Could Do Was Cry', 'My Dearest Darling', 'Stop the Wedding' – all made the pop charts, none of them doing much justice to her voice. Only with the release of 'Something's Got a Hold On Me', a pure Sanctified hoedown lifted directly from a gospel song, and a live album recorded in Nashville in 1964 did the earth mama re-emerge in all her raw, dare one say 'ballsy', glory. *Etta James Rocks the House* is her equivalent of Sam Cooke's Harlem Square album, emerging from the milksop pop nadir of early '60s America with raucous covers of Ray Charles's 'What'd I Say', Barrett Strong's 'Money', and Jimmy Reed's 'Baby, What You Want Me to Do', all recorded in front of a vociferous black audience. The voice is as tough as any man's, screaming blues murder over the band, phrasing with down-home abrasiveness ('any' is 'inneh', 'wings' is 'wangs'), and pointing forward to the gritty, bone-crunching sides cut in Muscle Shoals three years later.

The *Tell Mama* album Etta recorded at Rick Hall's Fame studio in 1967 remains a high-watermark of Southern Earth Mama soul, as notable for its pummelling up-tempo tracks

(Clarence Carter's title song, Otis Redding's 'Security') as for brooding ballads like 'I'd Rather Go Blind', 'The Love of My Man', and 'Don't Lose Your Good Thing'. There is nothing abject about the pain of 'I'd Rather Go Blind', refashioned by Jerry Wexler over a decade later on Etta's *Deep in the Night* album; rather something bleak, grave, almost parched of emotion. If the vocal is weary, even a little lazy, it makes more sense than histrionics ever could and stands to this day as one of her greatest performances. 'Tell Mama' speaks for itself, a Staxified, horn-blasted stomp that gives full vent to 'all this bitch shit inside me'. ('I let everything out,' she told me after coming offstage at the 1989 Montreux Jazz Festival, 'and then maybe I get back the security I need.')

Much of the material Etta recorded in the '70s and '80s plays rather self-consciously on her status as hard-bitten survivor. Of the albums she cut for Chess in the '70s, the best by far was *Come a Little Closer* (1974), recorded not long after she checked out of a horrendous detox at Tarzana Psychiatric Hospital in LA and including two junkie classics in 'Out on the Streets Again' – her equivalent to Esther Phillips's 'Home Is Where the Hatred Is' – and the extraordinary, wordless 'Feelin' Uneasy'. Richard Williams described the version of Randy Newman's 'Let's Burn Down the Cornfield' as 'one of the most sulphurously sexy records ever made', and it would have to be included among her swampiest, greasiest, downright *nastiest* performances. Finally, an arrangement of 'St Louis Blues' presents Etta as a modern-day Bessie Smith, bringing everything full circle in the earth mama stakes. The *Changes* album Allen Toussaint produced on her in New Orleans – scene of her Little Richard-style '50s classic 'Tough Lover' – was indifferently funky but boasted a superb ballad in its title track. ('I'm your part-time lover and your full-time fool', Etta spits with savage self-loathing.)

Deep in the Night employed crack sessionmen like Larry Carlton and Jeff Porcaro but only yielded up one great track, an improbably thrilling reading of the Eagles' 'Take It to the Limit' that features one of Etta's most barnstorming vocals and serves as a kind of country-gospel 'My Way' for her whole turbulent career. (The breathless, relentless howls at the end of the song have to be heard to be believed.) A decade later, she was rescued by another fairy godfather, Island's Chris Blackwell, who assigned her to that old Muscle Shoals workhorse Barry Beckett for the splendid *Seven Year Itch*. This was a gumbo of funk, rock, and country-soul, and a collection of classic southern songs to boot: Otis's 'I Got the Will', Bobby Charles's 'The Jealous Kind', and no less than three songs associated with that second-generation, ninety-nine-pound earth mama Ann Peebles ('Come to Mama', inevitably, 'How Strong Is a Woman', and a sublime version of 'Breaking Up Somebody's Home' – or *smashing* up somebody's home, as Etta has it in one of the choruses). If all the up-tempo stuff raged and howled as furiously as ever, the show was almost stolen by the last track, a plaintive Troy Seals ballad called 'One Night', which gave Etta free rein to try a little of her own kind of tenderness and ended up as one of the most gorgeous things she's ever done. In comparison, 1990's *Stickin' to My Guns* disappointed, with only a thunderous version of the Mable John classic 'Your Good Thing (Is About to End)' standing out.

As with Bobby Bland, Etta James's legacy is to be found primarily in the soul singers of the '60s and '70s: in her case, tough cookies like Laura Lee, Candi Staton, Gwen McCrae, and those two formidable Bettys, Harris and LaVette. It's unlikely that Tina Turner, Gladys Knight, Millie Jackson, or even Janis

Joplin would have been the singers they were without the influence of Etta and the earth mama tradition. Soul was the perfect home for these husky-voiced belters with their defiant, delirious songs of heartbreak and infidelity: Turner's Spector epic 'River Deep, Mountain High', Knight's furious, pre-Marvin Gaye stab at 'I Heard It Through the Grapevine', titanic Berns/Ragovoy creations like Lorraine Ellison's 'Stay With Me' and Erma Franklin's 'Piece of My Heart', together with lesser-known masterpieces like Doris Allen's primitive, lacerating 'Shell of a Woman' and Mattie Moultrie's volcanic rendition of 'That's How Strong My Love Is'. These are records which make the earth move.

Of the women who came up in the wake of Etta and her ilk, almost all came directly out of the church, and most returned to it at least intermittently. Mavis Staples's contralto was so deep and gravelly that when her father first formed the Staple Singers he made her the group's *bass* singer. It remains frighteningly powerful nearly forty years later, the sound of someone so ecstatically exhausted by the spirit that she seems to be gasping for air and heaving words out of her throat. As a teenager she idolized Dorothy Love Coates and Ruth Davis – 'the hardest female belter in gospel', according to Tony Heilbut – and developed her breathless phrasing along their lines. Her best years were the classic '50s of the Staple Singers' Vee Jay recordings, when Pop Staples played her off against his understated baritone and vibrato blues guitar; by the '70s, both with the Staples and as a solo artist, she sounded as if she was holding back for fear of letting go, cutting off phrases like a huskier Curtis Mayfield. More than most refugees from gospel she seems uncomfortable in the secular field, though you'd never guess it from the stupendous Brian and Eddie Holland production 'Love Gone Bad' (1983).

An equally fearsome contralto was that of Mitty Collier, whose 1965 Chess album *Shades of a Genius* was dominated by Ray Charles songs (hence the title) but also featured two remarkable ballads based on songs by Chicago luminary James Cleveland, 'I Had a Talk with My Man Last Night' and 'No Faith, No Love'. In her huge, dark voice there was something of Inez Andrews, a gospel high priestess whose statuesque, Amazonian features Collier shared, as well as of Nina Simone's precise, considered enunciation. Certainly there is nothing garbled or screamed in Mitty's sombre reading of 'Drown in My Own Tears', but if she rarely lets go or hollers she somehow suggests more emotion in the act of reining it in than do most singers belting it out. By the early '70s, when William Bell produced sessions of her in Atlanta, she was sounding more ragged and anguished: the version of Bell's own 'Share What You Got' is as deep as deep soul gets. Significantly, she lost her voice after recording the last side, and only regained it after returning permanently to gospel. *The Warning* (1972) featured the original 'I Had a Talk with My God Last Night'.

Laura Lee, who sang with Della Reese and ex-Caravan Cassietta George in her mother's group the Meditation Singers, followed in Collier's footsteps at Chess and achieved the same kind of husky sultriness on the jazzy James Cleveland song 'I Don't Need You'. In the main, though, her voice was a sharp, tough little instrument, beautifully suited to belting out warnings and solicitations like 'Dirty Man' and 'Wanted: Lover, No Experience Necessary'. Her best sides were cut during the post-Etta Chess invasion of Muscle Shoals, although she is more renowned today as the quasi-feminist bedroom rapper (and precursor of Millie Jackson) who recorded on Hot Wax. In the '80s Lee returned to gospel with the Al Green-produced *Jesus Is the Light of My Life*.

The most soulful and gospel-intense of the singers Allen Toussaint recorded in New Orleans in the '60s, Betty Harris was adopted by Big Maybelle as a maid/protégée in the late '50s and recorded by Bert Berns in 1963 on what is almost the definitive version of his song 'Cry to Me' – a performance of sensuous, almost maternal intimacy that builds irresistibly to the throaty rhetorical question 'Don't you feel like crying?' Much of Toussaint's material – 'Ride Your Pony', 'I'm Gonna Git Ya' – was too rhythmically quirky to provide space for her voice, but songs like 'What a Sad Feeling', 'What'd I Do Wrong', and the heavily gospel-infused 'Nearer to You' (as in 'Nearer My God to Thee . . .') were tailor-made for her harsh timbre and wild, jagged phrasing. Listen to 'I went from rags to riches since I met you' or 'You've used me but I still love you' in 'What'd I Do Wrong', where she fights to accommodate Toussaint's second-line rhythms and sounds possessed, deranged, by grief. On the funky duet 'A Fool for You' she met her male match in James Carr, for whom she is said to have worked temporarily as a road manager: a pity that this marriage of soul deities couldn't have been consummated in something a little more *tortured*.

Ann Peebles was Willie Mitchell's equivalent to Betty Harris, a slim, demure girl whose stark, brittle voice and careful phrasing have a curious coldness about them that is perfect for the unsentimental 'Part-time Love' and spookily forlorn on the likes of 'I Still Love You' (both 1970). 'Ancient and remorseless', Clive Anderson called it, and it sounded like a condemned soul caught between the church and the blues: never showy or abandoned, even on songs of vengeance like 'Breaking Up Somebody's Home' or 'I'm Gonna Tear Your Playhouse Down', and placing every phrase with unerring precision. Like all Mitchell's acts, she was always recorded without echo or reverb, a sound spare and naked as the truth, ringing with an eerie death rattle in the nose.

Candi Staton was the first home-grown female star to emerge at Muscle Shoals after Aretha Franklin and the Chess artists recorded there. With a voice like a hoarse, down-home Gladys Knight, she came straight out of the country church to belt up-tempo, Staple-ish songs like 'I'm Just a Prisoner', and in the process suffered at the hands of producer Rick Hall, who wanted to turn her into a female Wilson Pickett. By the time of her major hit, 'Young Hearts Run Free' (1974), she was free of Hall and playing a wise-before-her-years earth mama who counsels that 'self-preservation is what's really going on today'. Today she's back in gospel. Gwen McCrae, wife of 'Rock Your Baby' George, fell into the same bag and has always been a ludicrously overlooked singer. Based in Florida, she never had the luck to find a song like stablemate Betty Wright's 'Clean Up Woman' but managed nevertheless to record a smattering of superbly charged performances: '90% of Me Is You', the Latimore classic 'Let's Straighten It Out', versions of Bobby Bland's 'Lead Me On' and 'Ain't Nothing You Can Do', and her 1981 dancefloor masterwork 'Funky Sensation'. Tougher and haughtier than Staton's, her voice has exactly the same quality of inflamed desperation.

Gladys Knight herself remains one of the few truly great female singers ever to have recorded for Motown. Compared to the likes of Diana Ross she is superbly skilled, a glitzy earth mama whose big, warm, generous voice continues to redeem pieces of *schlock* like the James Bond theme 'Licence to Kill'. As a schmaltz-soul balladeer she has few equals, as anyone who knows the incredible 'Neither One of Us', or the version of Burt Bacharach's 'Seconds', will tell you. Listen as she builds from a smoky purr to a choking cry, by way of breathtaking anticipations, interpolations, and lustrous legato phrasing. The power and the control, together with the little cracks and tears which give the voice its edge, are astonishing.

Betty LaVette was a backwoods Etta James, with a tomboyish, inimitably abrasive timbre roughly comparable to the Lulu who recorded at Muscle Shoals in the late '60s. On her classic sides, like the ghostly 'Let Me Down Easy' (1965), the swampy 'He Made a Woman Out of Me' (1969), and the bitterly reproachful 'Your Turn to Cry' (1972), she is among the very greatest exponents of sandpaper soul, with her pinched vowels and snarling delivery. Irma Thomas and Barbara Lynn were altogether less assertive examples of the earth mama: as Charlie Gillett observed, Lynn demonstrated 'a sense of serenity and warmth that was rare for the period', and neither of them could ever be accused of belting. Irma sang with a breathy, dreamy solicitation, sharing a certain clipped style of phrasing with New Orleans colleague Betty Harris. 'Anyone Who Knows What Love Is', recorded on the West Coast, sounds entranced, almost drugged in its wistfulness, while her version of 'I Need Your Love So Bad' is easily the female equal of Willie John's dazed, diffident original. At Muscle Shoals, on songs like Otis Redding's 'Good to Me', she sounded simultaneously dreamy and defiant, the voice at one moment breaking, squeaking, the next floating off on an airy sigh of contentment. Barbara's husky alto and eccentric, exaggerated phrasing were magical on the early swamp-soul ballad 'You'll Lose A Good Thing' and on later country-soul songs such as 'People Like Me': at times she could have been a more restrained Randy Crawford.

What, finally, of the *white* earth mama, inheriting the blowzy mantle of Sophie Tucker and Mildred Bailey? Listen to the huge, ringing contralto of Timi Yuro, whose hits in the first half of the '60s were produced by Dinah Washington cohort Clyde Otis, and tell me it isn't a black voice: an Italian take, in fact, on Dinah and her greatest disciple Esther Phillips. (Like Esther, Yuro cut an album of country songs, turning Hank Snow's 'I'm Movin' On' into an up-tempo R&B stomper that knocks spots off Ray Charles's version.) Dusty Springfield has always been overrated as a soul singer, her voice a limited and often irritatingly breathy instrument, but at her best – on the 1969 album recorded in Memphis, for example – she exudes a parched, Peggy Lee-ish sensuality, a peroxide blackness that remains mildly affecting.

The ultimate white soul mama, of course, was Janis Joplin, a tiny Texan with bad skin and a finger permanently hovering over the self-destruct button. Janis hightailed it off to hippie capital San Francisco as soon as she could, but for all her spaced-out posturings in Big Brother and the Holding Company the down-home Texas grit spilled out every time she got behind a microphone. She was a honky Etta James, born to pour every ounce of her lust to be black through the 'mama' of her live version of 'Tell Mama'. Like Etta's, her low notes were almost mannish-boy tough: this was the especially harsh slant she gave to 'naw' or 'more'. The straight open-throat bawling I can take or leave, but there was another kind of rasp, one that scraped through the throat but sat in the roof of the mouth, and it sounded like a desert sandstorm howling over sun-bleached bones. If she worked too hard, and too messily, at filling every available space in her Berns/Ragovoy chestnuts – 'Cry Baby', 'Get It While You Can', and 'Piece of My Heart', the latter as much an anthem of hippie soul as Joe Cocker's 'With a Little Help from My Friends' – she never sounded phoney. Caught, like all her junkie earth mama idols, between haughty (bi)sexuality and pitiful loneliness, she used her voice as a channel of both release and self-abuse. On *Cheap Thrills*, Big Mama Thornton's 'Ball and Chain' – virtually an earth mama anthem

– becomes a primal scream session of mangled hollering and guitar distortion; more subtly, her revision of 'Little Girl Blue' (arranged by Gabriel Mekler, later to work with Etta James, no less) suggests a sense of isolation worthy of Esther Phillips.

Country Joe McDonald said Joplin was always asking if she would ever be as good a singer as Otis Redding or Tina Turner, and pianist Nick Gravenites is quoted in Myra Friedman's *Buried Alive* to the effect that 'she wanted to be respected as a great singer, not as a hippie freak'. It must have broken her heart when – the token honky – she flopped at the annual Stax Records Revue in late 1968. The fact remains that nobody has ever sounded anything like her – so crazed, so frantic, so remote – and that no white female has ever broken so much ground singing the black earth mama blues.

V

Redneck Soul

George Jones and the White Man's Blues

No one is fonder of saying that country music is 'the white man's blues' than black artists like B. B. King, Etta James, and Bobby Womack. Few people, moreover, have paid higher tributes to singers like Hank Williams, Patsy Cline, and George Jones than southern blacks who might be thought to abhor country music and all that it stands for. Musically, at least, there is the tacit black recognition that a greater country singer might have as much to say about joy and pain and life and death as the greatest blues or soul voices – and, further, that the likes of Williams, Cline, and Jones all possessed supremely 'soulful' voices.

It is only comparatively recently, however, that the country voice has been taken at all seriously by 'rock' critics. Before the 'New Country' hype of the '80s, pundits and punters alike looked at country music the way *Easy Rider* looked at the American South in general: with disgust and shame. If people today take a mocking pleasure in the attitudes of a song like 'Stand By Your Man', few whites outside the South ever bothered to make much of a case for the vocal artistry of a Lefty Frizzell. Didn't all country artists sing in a constricted nasal whine, replete with redneck twang and hokey parochialism?

Actually, a lot of them did, and this urban rock attitude to the country voice was understandable. Where gospel and blues singers cry out in an animalistic expression of release, country singers rein in and control their slurs and idiosyncrasies: even great singers like George Jones only accent *within* the beat, rarely crying out *across* it. They might raise more hell and beat more wives than any bluesman ever did, but their singing has something almost anally retentive about it, a sense of clenched restraint rather than emotional effusion.

Nonetheless, within these constrictions, which have much to do with country's use of the voice as a narrative rather than explosive instrument, there is ample room for vocal play and 'grain'. As much as Robert Johnson or Little Willie John, for instance, Hank Williams sang in a raw, stinging voice that revelled in its own torment, twisting and contorting vowels into pinched moans and wails which sound as painfully beautiful as anything Billie Holiday ever recorded. Williams's sound seems to roll around his mouth from the throat to the nose, curling and undulating through pursed lips in perverse musical shapes. Cries are held with a keening, concentrated purity – the 'apart' of 'Cold, Cold Heart', the 'met' of 'Lost Highway' – but much of his phrasing consists of playful distortions: the bizarre yodel of 'Moaning the Blues' and 'Long Gone Lonesome Blues', for instance, or the 'low-wah-wonesome' of 'Lonesome Whistle'. If his lower range is jokey, almost Presleyian, the tenor timbre is pure blues-black, a marriage of hillbilly plaintiveness and honky-tonk swagger – or 'mountain blues and Delta soul', in Douglas

Green's words – that couldn't be further from the clearly crooned diction of an Eddy Arnold if its life depended on it. Williams claimed he was the musical offspring of Roy Acuff (the mountain wail) and Ernest Tubb (the honky-tonk phrasing), but the influence of his black boyhood mentor Rufus 'Tee-Tot' Payne probably had more to answer for.

An equally 'soulful', if more purely honky-tonk-based voice, was that of William Orville 'Lefty' Frizzell, whose influence can be heard as much in country-soul singers like Percy Sledge and Joe Simon as in the lugubriously mellow voices of Merle Haggard or Johnny Rodriguez. Frizzell claimed that his dreamy, lazily nasal drawl was the result of trying (unsuccessfully) to emulate the 'blue yodel' of his idol Jimmie Rodgers; more prosaically still, he said he simply got tired of holding high notes and let them 'roll down' instead of straining. Wherever it came from it was exquisite, sweeter and more fruitily resonant than Hank Williams's: a tenor that glides with blithe grace through gently reproachful honky-tonk ballads like 'Time Changes Things' and 'It Gets Late So Early'.

The greatest male voice in all of country, and a man who remains as much a 'singers' singer' as Frank Sinatra or Bobby Bland, is George Jones, like Lefty Frizzell a Texan from the honky-tonk oil-town heartlands around Beaumont and Port Arthur. Jones started out with the same backwoods gospel roots as Hank Williams, whose influence on the early Jones records for Starday ('Why Baby Why', 'No Money in This Deal', and others) was almost total. The spry, jaunty tenor one hears in an up-tempo side like 'Never Been So Weary' (1958) is very far from the George Jones on United Artists in the '60s or the alcoholic 'no-show' legend of the '70s, although the eccentric timing and exaggeratedly open vowels (as in 'grim' and 'sigh') of gospel songs like 'Cup of Loneliness' (1957) are inimitably Jonesian.

Like Hank Williams, Jones had a foot in both the hillbilly and honky-tonk camps: the voice was essentially rural, one might even say *fundamentalist*, while the songs reflected the industrial atmosphere of east Texas as embodied in the influences of Ernest Tubb, Floyd Tillman, and others. By the early '60s, after a stint on Mercury Records, he had developed a vocal sound and style which took Hank's tortured delivery into another dimension, a voice which turned brilliantly ironical songs like 'She Thinks I Still Care' and 'A Girl I Used to Know' into definitive country masterpieces. No one has ever sung quite like Jones: as John Morthland observed, he appears to do it from a completely different *place* to other singers. 'The voice', Morthland wrote, 'seems to rise from the knots in his stomach, the words seeping out through clenched teeth . . .', and Doug Green and Bob Oermann called it 'an out-of-the-body voice almost frightening in its eloquence'. Unlike other post-Hank singers – Webb Pierce, for example, with his tight nasal vibrato – Jones's voice is a rich swirl of sound, a weird blend of tenor and baritone at one moment densely concentrated and the next airily diffuse. Oscillating permanently between sharp iteration and what Mark Rose called 'a sleepy ache', it burrows in and out of itself: its 'i' and 'ee' vowels are all but swallowed at the back of the mouth, and words are bent, pressed, squeezed, even choked into mad shapes. In 'She Thinks I Still Care', 'idea' becomes 'ideooo'; 'such as I' in 'Lonely Street' becomes 'sichazoi'; and more generally, Jones-friendly words like 'free' and 'dream' swell with jaw-clenched intensity, stretched as far as they will go before being strung together. Biographer Bob Allen talked of a 'whining emotional ambivalence and mock sadness', and there's usually a kind of clowning element, a swaying unsteadiness, in the vocal path. What is beautiful is how one can never predict whether he's going to wail or sigh, bawl or whisper. It is more like the bowing of a fiddle player than the diction of a singer.

Like so many others, the voice has deepened and mellowed over the years, though in Jones's case it is now more eccentric and hillbilly-inflective than ever. For over two decades producer Billy Sherrill, the mastermind behind Jones's one-time wife Tammy Wynette, has cushioned it in a spacious and luxurious bed of Nashville sound, and if much of the time the effect is one of coasting, the occasional startling moment redeems their somewhat play-safe collaboration. His 'comeback' hit of 1980, 'He Stopped Loving Her Today', was an unabashed Kleenex job – in Jones's own words, 'a sad, slobbery tear-jerker' – but it extracted from him a performance of almost vertiginous beauty, with every phrase, every minuscule change in mood, plotted to perfection. Another Curly Putman song, '(Couldn't Love Have Picked) A Better Place to Die' (1981) was Jones at his rawest and most chokingly vulnerable.

Few other country voices can stand comparison with that of George Jones, though for sheer harmonic beauty it would be hard to beat male duos like the Stanley Brothers and the Louvin Brothers, purveyors of that aching mountain music known as 'the high, lonesome sound'. Here vocal 'play' is kept to a minimum, with voices blending in pure, flawlessly sustained cries. On the distaff side, that contemporary mother-and-daughter team, the Judds, have recorded a classic of the duo genre in the magical 'Maybe Your Baby's Got the Blues'. Among other solo artists, Willie Nelson's dry, reedily ruminative tone possesses a curious, almost a-musical power, as does the thin and wavering sound of Gram Parsons, whose pitching was suspect at the best of times but whose voice touches me with its wasted fragility. If Charlie Rich is a country singer at all, it is really in the same sense that Ray Charles, another maverick magpie who fuses gospel, blues, jazz, and country into one hybrid style, is a country singer. Technically he's far from great – somewhere between schmaltzy Presley and mellow Joe Simon – but on gloriously remorseful songs like 'Feel Like Going Home', 'My Elusive Dreams', and 'Pieces of My Life' he is peculiarly affecting.

Was Elvis Presley – Elvis the hillbilly cat – a great singer? Certainly the primal rockabilly voice of the 1954 Sun sides is an interesting one, if only because it brings together so many different stylistic strands: honky-tonk, white gospel, crooning balladry, Delta blues, and the operatic sobbing of Roy Brown and company. A one-man melting pot, Presley heard blues singers in Tupelo, Mississippi, attended the black East Trigg Baptist Church in Memphis, worshipped Billy Eckstine and Dean Martin, and sang the songs of Bill Monroe and Hank Snow. When he put it all together it galvanized a nation into mass hysteria. From the very start, when he wandered into Sam Phillips's Memphis Recording Service to make a vanity recording in the summer of 1953, it was a voice which – in the words of Phillips's assistant Marion Keisker – 'changed every eight bars', jumping from gurgling baritone to whining tenor in the space of a line and wreaking playful havoc with the Ink Spots' 'My Happiness'. Both Keisker and Phillips noted that he was 'a good ballad singer', which is a curiously mundane description, but Presley himself admitted that he had never sung anything but 'slow music and ballads' before 1954. (As Henry Pleasants noted, on 'It's Now Or Never', adapted from the Italian song 'O Sole Mio', he sounds 'for all the world like a Neapolitan tenor'.)

Ballads provided some of the vocal highlights in the Sun sessions. Think of the spectral 'Blue Moon' – used to brilliant effect in Jim Jarmusch's film *Mystery Train* – with Presley's tremulous falsetto moans floating through Sam Phillips's echo chamber. Drawing on Billy Eckstine's 1948 version of the song, it shows how completely at ease Elvis was with Tin Pan Alley material, and how entranced he could sound at that tempo. On the proto-rockabilly treatments of Bill Monroe's 'Blue Moon of Kentucky' and Roy Brown's 'Good Rockin' Tonight', his energy and timing are joyous and infectiously witty, breathlessly self-preening and verging on high camp: Gary Giddins called it 'minstrelsy' and Jackie Wilson parodied it on 'Reet Petite'. Country singer Bob Luman caught an early show and decided he would never again try to sing like Webb Pierce or Lefty Frizzell.

As the voice aged, it lost its pliancy and elasticity and became increasingly hammy. The quivering vibrato soon sounded laboured and histrionic, taking on an artificially baritonal depth and resonance. Even on the great return-to-Memphis sessions of 1969, which yielded 'In the Ghetto' and 'Suspicious Minds', the voice is a sated, decadent instrument. Producer Chips Moman recalled that every time he told Presley he was off pitch 'his whole entourage would nearly faint'. (Coincidentally, Roy Hamilton, one of Elvis's great sobbing idols, was in the same studio at the time, and Elvis watched him at work. He also recorded Clyde McPhatter's sob classic 'Without Love' with Moman.)

In the annals of the white man's blues, it is worth mentioning a few honorary rednecks whose voices, pitched somewhere between country and soul, have always meant a lot to me. That bastion of Texan R&B tradition Delbert McClinton manages to do more with his hoarse, road-weary pipes than do most white blues pretenders, probably because he's been doing it since he was fifteen years old. If the major part of his repertoire is made up of boozy, 'red-eyed-blue-eyed' rhythm'n'blues, his readings of country-soul ballads like 'The Jealous Kind' or Otis Redding's

'I've Got Dreams to Remember' showcase a cracked, aching voice that seems closer to Etta James than to any comparable male singers. (Interesting that they've both been produced by Barry Beckett, and that both have recorded 'The Jealous Kind' and the Temptations' 'Shaky Ground'.) The combination of snarling black timbre and classic Texan inflection is as irresistible on the funk of 'Love Rustler' or 'Hold On to Your Hiney' as it is on the honky-tonk country of 'Two More Bottles of Wine' and 'Victim of Life's Circumstances'. From the orthodox blue-eyed soulisms of his '60s sides for Le Cam, reminiscent of fellow Texan Roy Head, to the ravaged voice of 1989's *Live in Austin*, is some journey.

The three singers in that extraordinary group The Band – Levon Helm, Rick Danko, and the late Richard Manuel – all possessed beautiful quasi-country voices, as the inclusion of Lefty Frizzell's 'Long Black Veil' on the group's first album *Music from Big Pink* (1968) made clear. That four-fifths of them hailed from Canada, and furthermore came out of an intellectual rock context (read association with Bob Dylan), now seems almost irrelevant: as their guitarist and songwriter Robbie Robertson said, what they played was 'mountain music'. The three voices, all of them resonating with rural America's long history, were similar enough to trade lines seamlessly and blend into one harmonic whole – listen to the three of them on *Stage Fright*'s desperately moving 'The Rumour' – but where Helm was capable of a certain jollity, Danko (on 'It Makes No Difference', for instance) and Manuel (on 'Whispering Pines') seemed haunted by grief and loneliness.

Even Bruce Springsteen might justify inclusion as an 'honorary redneck': he's not a great singer by any reckoning, but increasingly I have found myself touched and stirred by acoustic, pseudo-'country' songs like 'One Step Up' and 'Cautious Man' (both from the somewhat underrated *Tunnel of Love* album). As with all special country voices there is an indefinable 'grain' here, a grain of emotional truth both gritty and stoically sad.

Can white men sing the blues? The answer must be a muted yea, sung through clenched teeth in a 'high, lonesome' voice.

VI

Preachers and Balladeers

The Southern Soul Men

Solomon Burke and the Soul Clan

The southern Soul Man has a special place in the pantheon of black vocal artists. He is the heavyweight, the voice with the bigger punch. If *les femmes*, too, have their KO voices, the Soul Man's special power comes precisely – paradoxically – from the breaking of his male strength and dignity, from his being reduced to the abjection of a child. Otis Redding was 'Mr Soul' because he was a big broad-shouldered ox with a 'a li'l pain in my heart' that made him choke and splutter. We love this humbling of the Soul Man, the Mr Pitiful archetype, because it permits us the vicarious sensation of dropping our cool and releasing our own pain. The church-reared Soul Man of the '60s is the most potent symbol of this catharsis available to us. In him all the vanities and fripperies of showbiz have been stripped away, leaving only an anonymous figure in a sweat-soaked suit and a voice of elemental woe.

We turn this pain into something heroic, Herculean. Just as

gospel singers like Archie Brownlee and Julius Cheeks were rated according to their ability to 'wreck the church', so the 'greatest' Soul Man is he who, as a spectacle of heartbreak, most debases himself. Hence the temptation to excess, exaggeration, self-parody – to cross what Henry Pleasants called 'the thin line between ecstasy and exhibitionism'. Already it is a soul cliché that in his last year or two Otis Redding was parodying himself to death.

Ironically, the first great 'Southern Soul Man' wasn't southern at all: he was born in Philadelphia and recorded, at least initially, in New York. Nor was Solomon Burke a singer who ever got *carried away* in the sense that Otis or Wilson Pickett did; there was an uncanny degree of control in even his wildest cries. But Burke, dubbed the 'Wonder Boy Preacher' before he'd so much as reached puberty, paved the way for a soul style made up of equal parts preaching and balladeering, and in his wake came all the great male voices recorded in Memphis and Muscle Shoals.

Burke's voice was an eccentric mêlée of inclinations: to pure gospel, to the pseudo-religious pop bombast of Roy Hamilton, and – by way of Brook Benton – to the mannered baritonal phrasing of Nat King Cole. Groomed in pre-soul days almost as a Harry Belafonte, the portly boy was hardly a rhythm'n'blues shouter, yet the timbre of the voice was raw enough for his first Atlantic hit, of all things a country song, to be retrospectively proclaimed the first '60s 'soul' record. 'Just Out of Reach' (1961) was an immaculate performance boasting the entire ragbag of vocal tricks and trademarks that would characterize his recorded *oeuvre* over the next twenty years: the sweetly refined diction, the lilting, considered grace of his phrasing, the leisurely flattenings, the minimal melisma at the end of the lines, like an internal shiver or implosion, and the sense that he is holding himself back and simply floating on the top of his voice. Even his cries are *contained* – nothing ever blasted out for the sake of it – and this is the essence of the pleasure in listening to him. Jerry Wexler, Solomon's mentor at Atlantic, says that in later years he was prone to laziness and 'oversouling', but few voices have been so restrained or controlled. If his inflamed screams sound like Tom Jones colliding with John Fogerty, and if the raging 'c-c-c-cry' of Bert Berns's immortal 'Cry to Me' was a decisive influence on Otis Redding's near-barking style, then some of his later ballad performances – like 'Time Is a Thief' (1968), 'What Am I Living For?' (1969), and the remarkable acoustic version of 'Drown in My Own Tears' (1972) – are barely whispered.

The voice is still there, as anyone who has heard the Rounder albums *Soul Alive!* (1985) and *A Change Is Gonna Come* (1986) will know. 'There is no one with a greater vocal range, not just of notes but of nuances and timbres,' said fellow Soul Clan member Don Covay, and the double live album affords one as much joy in his easy gliding between tenor and baritone ranges, between harsh rasps and sweet croons, as in his growly, evuncular, tongue-in-cheek preaching. As for the exquisite version of 'A Change Is Gonna Come', here once again he opts for control and subtlety, saving all the song's pain for one soaring falsetto moment in the final 'I been *so* afraid of living'.

A far more dionysian member of the 'Soul Clan' than either Burke or Covay – whose voice (out of its favoured falsetto range) was the principal influence on the young Mick Jagger – was wicked Wilson Pickett, a beautiful panther of a man with a searing scream that came straight from the throat of the Sensational Nightingales' Julius Cheeks. His ferocious voice had already been heard on the Falcons' 1961 hit 'I Found a Love' when he joined Solomon Burke on the Atlantic roster and kicked off a long series of Soul Man classics with the Stax-recorded 'In the Midnight Hour' (1965). Like James Brown's, it's a voice which operates on full-throttle at all times: there is nothing of Burke's shading or agility in the likes of 'Land of a Thousand Dances' or 'Funky Broadway'. But there is a certain guttural grandeur in its raw, bleeding-throat timbre, heard to best effect in the classic version of 'Hey Jude' and on ballads like 'Back in Your Arms' (both 1969). Pickett's great crony Bobby Womack – who, unlike the obstinate Pickett, played on the one and only Soul Clan single – not only wrote several hits for the Wicked One but sang like him too. It was a more introspective, complex Pickett that one heard in Womack's voice, however – part sexy Soul Man, part lay preacher, part pop-influenced singer–song-writer – and his music quickly outgrew Wilson's classic three-minute soul strutting. Womack's singing, with its wayward, semi-rapped phrasing, is all about timing: the placing of words in the flow of vocal rhythm. It's not beautiful, and certainly not elegant, this grizzly, growling, Satchmo-esque voice, but sparring with Patti Labelle on 1984's epic 'Love Has Finally Come At Last' its howling passion is nothing short of magnificent.

Next to Pickett or Otis Redding, Joe Tex was less a Soul Man than what Peter Guralnick called a 'clown prince', a court jester with the voice of a folksy, mischievous James Brown. He was closer to white country music than even Solomon Burke; closer, too, to the southern tradition of yarn-spinning songsters and jack-leg preachers. The persona conceived in 'Hold What You've Got' (1964) served Joe through all his best sides, while the hoarse, chuckling voice combined Brown's rasp with Burke's playfully slurred diction. Like Womack's, it was hardly beautiful, but Tex more than made up for that with the ribald, didactic humour of his country-soul sermonettes.

Besides Arthur Conley, who took Otis Redding's place in the

Clan and is mentioned in a later section of this chapter, the sole remaining member of the Soul Clan was ex-Drifter Ben E. King, drafted in to replace Pickett on 'Soul Meeting'/'That's How It Feels' (1968) and probably the most 'uptown' member of the group. As with Solomon Burke, the voice of 'Save the Last Dance for Me', 'Spanish Harlem', and 'Stand By Me' combined raw tone with polished New York phrasing, and reached its peak in that violently impassioned Bert Berns production 'It's All Over'.

If the Soul Clan was something of a travesty – far from being a 'Soul Meeting', none of the five singers was in the studio at the same time – it brought together, however spuriously, some of the great Soul Men on Atlantic, and thirteen years later, with the ill-tempered Pickett coming back in to replace Arthur Conley, they re-gathered for a shambolic concert in New York. 'There *is* such a thing as a satisfied soul man,' Joe Tex told author Gerri Hirshey backstage, but clearly the Wicked One was not the example he had in mind.

Mr Soul: Otis Redding

'I Love You More Than Words Can Say', said Otis Redding – and words, in Rainer Maria Rilke's phrase, 'always melt into something beyond their embrace'.

Otis tried to embrace too much with his big, barking words and ended up saying very little. I'm not sure that I wasn't affected as a teenager by the way he was presented to me as Mr Soul, so that all I hear is this gruff, cracked baritone marked 'soul', but the fact is that his voice, trumpeting its needs like his early model and fellow Georgian Little Richard, had none of the shading or suppleness of his subsequent hero Sam Cooke. If the classic early ballads – 'These Arms of Mine', 'Pain in My

Heart' – are sung with admirable care and economy, later sides sound like an elephant trying to tiptoe on eggshells, a big ox maddened by a 'li'l pain'.

To be sure, the sound is hugely resonant, but its phrasing is too coarse and jagged to afford much pleasure. (The cry as he stretches to reach the horns in 'I've Been Loving You Too Long' may be hard to bear, but that doesn't make it great singing.) There is little melismatic skill to speak of, as a quick comparison of his 'A Woman, a Lover, a Friend' with Jackie Wilson's original will make clear, and when Otis tries to soften his delivery it merely becomes thin and airy. It's no wonder that shortly before his death he had to have polyps removed from his throat: any singing teacher will tell you that Redding's open-throated bawling, especially on his favourite 'stomp' songs, is vocal suicide.

There are modest successes in slow ballads like 'Good to Me' and 'My Lover's Prayer', but trickier songs like 'A Change Is Gonna Come' tend to make him overdo things. The phrasing here betrays a clumsy over-elaboration – not pretentious, merely erring on the side of generosity – and the little sub-Cookeian flutters sound like attempts at compensating for the basic coarseness of the timbre. On the version of 'For Your Precious Love' his vocal somersaults are worthy of an earnest white soulboy.

James Carr and the Country-Soul Ballad

A far greater singer, who took his cue from Redding's early ballad style and recently had critics the world over proclaiming him the greatest of all Soul Men, was James Carr, who recorded fourteen singles for the Memphis label Goldwax, then more or less disappeared from the business. True, sides like 'Dark End of the Street', 'Love Attack', and 'That's the Way Life Turned

Out for Me' were hardly major soul hits, but then Carr, a paralytically shy, even disturbed man, was hardly a natural star.

It is not outrageous to claim that Carr's is the greatest of all male southern soul voices. Certainly only Solomon Burke has sounded so raw, so *inflamed*, while maintaining such effortless control. Carr's is a deep, rich baritone, not plummily nasal like Percy Sledge's, more an elastic instrument that manages to leap from the velvety croon of a Joe Simon to the hoarse, frenzied shrieks of a Wilson Pickett. Its resonance is as cavernous as Bobby Bland's, its shadings and undulations almost subterranean. 'The way this guy sang really made goose pimples break out all over me,' said his original mentor Roosevelt Jamison. 'His voice was one of both humility and power.'

Jamison found Carr singing in a gospel group called the Harmony Echoes, and it's raw gospel passion you hear in these records, a voice of agonized yearning to be made whole, to be one with the beloved. At its most intense the hurt is positively frightening, with the voice sounding as if it's about to splinter in its pain. Every line of these songs is delivered with a burning, livid intensity, every word wrenched from the throat and yet placed with superb precision. The artistry is thrilling; the timing leaves Redding and Pickett trailing in the dust. Where other Soul Men get lazy, Carr is invariably tight, subtle, instinctively careful. Even when the voice frays and tears in the last gasped bars of his ballads, there is a tormented kind of control at work, a reining-in of abandon. 'James Carr had an emotional power that really stirred me up,' says Chips Moman, who co-wrote 'Dark End of the Street' with that blue-eyed soul legend Dan Penn. 'I could have sat and listened to him all day. He never got anywhere near what he should have been, which is an all-time great.'

So why wasn't/isn't James Carr an official all-time great?

Partly, I think, because he didn't want it, because, as Roosevelt Jamison says, he was 'kinda slow and childlike', ill-equipped to handle the cut-throat business of touring and promoting. 'James was very reserved, a real religious-type person,' recalls Quinton Claunch, his Goldwax producer. 'It was hard to get a conversation out of him.' But also because the passion of his records was too real, too naked, to cross over in the way his peers did.

The downfall of this mighty innocent, this holy fool who spoke in such awesome tongue, is recounted in depressing detail by Peter Guralnick, who, in the course of researching his book *Sweet Soul Music* (1986), found Carr 'practically narcoleptic' in a south Memphis housing project. When DJ Andy Kershaw tracked him down in 1987, he was semi-coherent but couldn't recall what he'd been doing for twenty years. Drugs had unquestionably played their part in his disintegration, but there is, and always has been, a more fundamental instability there. The '70s began for him with the promise of a big deal with Capitol, but a jail sentence in Florida soon put paid to that. Atlantic had him for one reasonable side, 'I'll Put It to You', but never followed it up. The only support over the years has come from Roosevelt Jamison, who produced him on one independently financed single in 1977 – the voice was still there even if all the marbles weren't – and two years later took him to Japan. (The mini-tour was cut short when Carr took too many of his anti-depressants and became spellbound onstage.) Today he is as desperate and bereft of hope as he always sounded in those records, a monstrous talent incapable of expressing itself.

Is James Carr the greatest of all the southern Soul Men? I think perhaps yes. For all the other worthy claimants to such a throne – and there are several equally obscure names among them – I know of no voice quite so dauntingly, shockingly powerful.

Of the other great country-soul balladeers, Carr's Goldwax labelmate Spencer Wiggins was the closest in vocal texture to the voice of 'Dark End of the Street', combining James's rich resonance with the phrasing of Johnny Adams and the high wailing of Jerry Ragovoy's protégé Howard Tate. On '(Take Me) Just As I Am', 'The Power of a Woman', and a version of Aretha's 'I Never Loved a (Wo)Man', he sounded like a more frantic, abrasive version of Carr, certainly far wilder in timbre and delivery than the smoothly mellow baritones of Joe Simon or Freddie North.

Joe Simon's velvet-smooth timbre and dreamy, languid phrasing – exemplified on sides like 'Nine Pound Steel' and the big 1969 hit 'The Chokin' Kind' – epitomize '60s country soul, borrowing apparently as much from the diffident inflections of a Lefty Frizzell as from the supper-club crooning of his early influence Arthur Prysock. He was a countrypolitan Jerry Butler, with a fluent and graceful voice that opened out from full, booming baritone to a nasal near-tenor. Even more lugubrious was Freddie North, who showed how closely he was following in Simon's steps by cutting 'Yours Love' as well as another country hit, Johnny Paycheck's 'She's All I Got', both of them featured on the Swamp Dogg-produced album *Friend*. But the undisputed cornball king of country soul was Percy Sledge, whose richly plummy, plaintively nasal, supremely unsophisticated voice all but cornered the market in mournful balladeering and periodically touched greatness: there aren't many '60s soul ballads that can stand with 'Out of Left Field' and 'Take Time to Know Her', or with 'I'll Be Your Everything' (1974) and 'You Had To Be There' (1983), for that matter. Recently an album of straight country songs, produced by Percy's long-time manager David Johnson, brought the whole country-soul story full circle, with the vocal power undimmed on versions of

George Jones's 'She Thinks I Still Care' and Lefty Frizzell's 'If You've Got the Money, I've Got the Time'. In an age of suave Mr Right mannerists, his almost unadorned phrasing – a voice which is just pure ache, pure love – remains extraordinary.

A very different kind of country-soul voice was that of the New Orleans singer Johnny Adams, who sang gospel with Bessie Griffin's Consolators before teaming up with a young Mac Rebennack (aka Dr John) to record Ric sides like the classic 'I Won't Cry' (1959) and 'A Losing Battle' (1962), a blues ballad featuring the sleepiest horn arrangement imaginable. Adams's commanding tenor sounded nothing like his New Orleans contemporaries, nor was it remotely comparable to the plaintive Alabama ache of Percy Sledge. In fact, with its stiff phrasing and shimmering vibrato, it combined an operatic sweep with the jazzy timbre of a Lou Rawls. Only his distinctive trademark, the occasional soaring into a shrieking falsetto register – hence his nickname the Tan Nightingale – let loose something more vulnerable.

Johnny's country-soul sides, spanning from 'Release Me' and 'Reconsider Me' in the late '60s to 'Hell Yes, I Cheated' and Conway Twitty's 'After All the Good Is Gone' in the '80s, are slightly reminiscent, right down to the falsetto, of Joe Hinton's 1964 treatment of the Willie Nelson classic 'Funny How Time Slips Away', but where Hinton sounds warm and involved, Adams always keeps his distance, maintaining a cold, grave dignity which is nonetheless extraordinarily hypnotic. On 1984's *From the Heart*, Boston's Rounder Records brought out the jazz in his voice – including a formidable scat passage and an astonishing 'mouth trombone' solo – and thus gave Johnny the chance to shine at last as something more than a soul balladeer.

Beautiful Screamers (reprise)

If James Carr and the (predominantly baritonal) country-soul balladeers were one side of the southern Soul Man coin, then the gritty, gravelly tenor voices of singers like O. V. Wright were the other. The grit and gravel in question had been sifted down from Archie Brownlee and the hard gospel screamers through the James Brown of 'Please, Please, Please' and 'Try Me', and if we are more inclined these days to see Brown as the godfather of dance music than as an R&B balladeer, that doesn't change the fact that his harsh, scraping voice was once as much at home in the sweet surrounds of 'I Want You So Bad' and 'I Love You, Yes I Do' – not to mention 'Prisoner of Love' and 'It's a Man's, Man's, Man's World' – as in the funk of 'Papa's Got a Brand New Bag'.

It was the pure, raw intensity of Brown's voice which almost single-handedly carried R&B beyond the mellifluous sobbing of his labelmates Clyde McPhatter and Jackie Wilson. He may not – by his own admission, no less – have been the singer that Little Willie John was, but for sheer primitive gospel power none of his contemporaries came close to 'Please, Please, Please' (1956). There are ten seconds in this song where James is simply coughing out the word 'I' over and over again, as though he's got something caught in his throat.

Brown's singing is distinctive because the *passion* of his voice is a peculiarly cold and hard one. He was a ball of energy but not one that whipped up warmth or any good-humoured sensuality. He had no *personality* in the sense that his fellow Georgian Little Richard had personality – think of that strangely frozen expression, that fixed frenzy and monkey smile. Yet within its limitations the voice had dynamics: listen to any of his ballad performances and hear devotion cracking into outrage, dulcet trills rolling into vicious yells. And nowhere is his vocal play more feverishly intricate than on the classic *Live at the Apollo Vol. 1*.

Like James Carr, Overten Vertis Wright was guided into the secular field by Roosevelt Jamison, who brought the pair of them to see Goldwax boss Quinton Claunch one night and whose classic ballad 'That's How Strong My Love Is' provided OV with his one and only Goldwax release. Unlike Carr, OV had already made records as lead singer of gospel group the Sunset Travelers, even enjoying regional success in the late '50s with 'On Jesus' Program' on Don Robey's Peacock label. The voice, moreover, was already completely formed by this stage, a pitch-perfect 'beautiful scream' you can trace all the way back through Archie Brownlee to R. H. Harris of the Soul Stirrers. Willie Mitchell, who produced him on Back Beat and Hi, called him 'the greatest singer who ever lived' – this from the man who discovered Al Green! – and only Pops Harris's great disciple Sam Cooke ever fused the rough with the smooth as perfectly, or sang with such ridiculous ease.

Kip Lornell, in his study of Memphis gospel, describes OV's voice as an 'ornamented' quartet lead, utilizing melisma, falsetto, and sforzando (or special emphasis on particular words), but if its whole approach derives directly from Archie Brownlee its unique 'grain' involves something less uniformly abandoned and more idiosyncratically mournful. Brownlee never floated or hovered in the way Wright does, sustaining long phrases with Sam Cooke's flowing smoothness, nor did he take such pleasure in his phrasing and enunciation, packing words into the shortest spaces, jumping octaves within a single bar, lisping on his 's's, blowing on the 'w's in a phrase like 'when you whisper', and connecting lines with little cries.

His finest moments are invariably on bleak gospel-blues

ballads like 'This Hurt Is Real' or that great 'jury of love' saga 'Eight Men, Four Women', harrowing lamentations in which a doleful female chorus wails behind his racked, sandpapered tenor. If some of his Houston-recorded sides share the '60s feel and style of his labelmate Bobby Bland, it is instructive to compare their respective versions of 'I'll Take Care of You': where Bland's is serenely solicitous, OV manages to make even this song of tender devotion sound grief-crazed, replete with one particularly blood-curdling falsetto howl.

When Willie Mitchell took over – you can hear the Hi sound beginning to come through on the Don Bryant song 'I Want Everyone to Know' – Wright got funkier on mid-tempo material and softer, more Al Green-like on ballads. But then even the pumping, disco-era 'Into Something (I Can't Shake Loose)' sounded vocally like a Baptist threnody, and the more immured OV became by a serious drug problem the more desperate he sounded on vinyl. (The man singing on the 1978 LP *The Bottom Line*, cut two years before his death from a heart attack, has clearly lost a couple of front teeth.) 'Soon I will be done with the trouble of this world,' he moaned on the gospel traditional 'I'm Going Home (to Live with God)', and he sounded like he was busting to get out of it.

A much less subtle and satisfying singer than O. V. Wright, but one who was nonetheless very close to him in the gospel-grit-and-gravel tenor range, was Otis Clay, a fellow Hi artist who excelled on funky material like 'Too Many Hands' and 'Trying to Live My Life Without You' – his 'Pouring Water On A Drowning Man' was better even than James Carr's – while never doing anything terribly interesting with ballads: too often, even on the wonderful 'It Was Jealousy', he sounds like he's straining, struggling to do what OV could do in his sleep. Another big Memphis O, Ollie Nightingale (ne Hoskins), stayed in gospel until 1968, when his Dixie Nightingales went secular with the funky Stax hit 'I Got a Sure Thing'. 'OV could literally make you cry,' he says of the man whose progress in the sinner's world he was carefully monitoring, and if his own high, needle-sharp tenor was less tear-jerking it was still a strange and intriguing instrument. Influenced by Ira Tucker and the Pilgrim Travelers' Kylo Turner – 'Tucker was so intelligent and polished, but Turner had that deep-down soul thing that I wanted' – Ollie sang tortured ballads like 'Standing on Your Promise' in a voice whose wild shriek of a scream didn't change the fact that it had a curiously feminine ring and intonation. (Amusing, then, that his best sides were songs of slighted macho pride like 'May the Best Man Win' and 'Here I Am Again'.) He's had a rough ride since his brief moment of Stax glory: 1983's *Troubled in Mind*, with its ultra-cheapo James Bennett production, had a sleeve-note thanking a friend for 'encouraging me not to quit when all seemed so hopeless', and when I saw him perform in Memphis in 1985 he'd been reduced to singing supper-club blues for tourists.

Oscar Toney Jr, yet another Big O, had a scream so bitterly harsh it couldn't have been construed as 'beautiful' by the most cloth-eared soul devotee in the world. But his raw, gloriously rural-sounding howl had a certain compelling charm about it, ill-suited as it was to uptown pop-soul songs like 'Any Day Now' and 'He Will Break Your Heart', and went hand in hand with the backwoods sermonettes which prefaced his readings of 'For Your Precious Love' and 'Without Love (There Is Nothing)'. If he never managed the melismatic curlicues of an O. V. Wright, the voice of his classic Capricorn side 'Down on My Knees' (1971) marks some kind of outpost on the wilder shores of primitive southern soul.

Equally gravelly if more polished than Oscar Toney Jr, the

'60s disciples of Sam Cooke all possessed 'beautiful screams'. One of them, Louis Williams of Goldwax vocal group the Ovations, even made a career out of sounding *exactly* like Sam, and furthermore was blessed with a series of delightful Cooke-style songs – 'It's Wonderful to Be in Love', 'I Believe I'll Go Back Home' and others – on which he could perfect his simulation. (Jackie Wilson has a similarly uncanny *doppelgänger* in Howard Huntsberry of the group Klique.) Less slavish as imitators were Johnnie Taylor, who replaced Sam in the Soul Stirrers before becoming one of his protégés at SAR Records in the early '60s; Arthur Conley, a protégé in turn of Cooke devotee Otis Redding; and Willie Hightower. Taylor's tough, pugnacious little voice was never in the Cooke or OV league but it had its own gritty, cheeky character and sounded equally good on bluesy Hayes/Porter songs like 'I Got to Love Somebody's Baby', funky hits like 'Who's Makin' Love', and '80s soul like the mighty 'Just Ain't Good Enough'. Conley and Hightower both adapted the frayed, coarsely sweet Cooke voice to the demands of the southern soul ballad: Willie sounded like Sam after a night on the tiles and often featured a Cooke medley in his live repertoire.

There is one freakish white voice which can stand with all these gravelly black screamers, and it belongs to an infamous southern soul legend who, according to Jerry Wexler, 'was always going to be next year's big thing'. By the time Eddie Hinton did finally get around to making a record, he was a disturbed, drunken wreck of his former boyish self who needed all Jerry Wexler's godfatherly powers of patronage to be allowed near a studio at all. But what a record *Very Extremely Dangerous* (1978) is: a scorching album of R&B and soul featuring perhaps the blackest white voice ever committed to vinyl, the result of hours of tortured screaming and obsessive imitation of his idols

Otis Redding, Wilson Pickett, and Bobby Womack. (You can hear Eddie yelping along on Bobby's 'A Little Bit Salty', which he wrote.) Redding in particular haunts the album – a version of 'Shout Bamalama' apes Otis's early Little Richard style brilliantly – while Womack's cosmic lay-preaching is readily detectable on the beautiful 'Get Off in It'.

Hinton had worked as a songwriter and session guitarist around Muscle Shoals and Memphis for several years before drugs and alcohol took their toll on his considerable promise. 'Eddie got in on the LSD trips,' recalls Dan Penn, 'and it messed him up. Something snapped up there, and he sort of got an obsession with sounding like Otis.' 'I started out singin' like Otis to try to get to sing like Sam Cooke,' Hinton told me when I tracked him down in 1985 in Decatur, Alabama, 'but I just kinda dropped the Cooke thing. I like Shirley Caesar, Joe Tex, and Wilson Pickett, that's the main sound I try to stay with.' If he wasn't doing himself any favours with his throaty screaming, the angrily abrasive howl it produced is undeniably thrilling, and sounds as good as ever on the mid-'80s Muscle Shoals recordings included on the Swedish LP *Letters From Mississippi*. Meanwhile, *Very Extremely Dangerous* continues to grow in reputation as a cult album, as Dave Marsh discovered when he found Nils Lofgren and cronies singing along to it backstage after a show on the *Born In The USA* tour. They were as dumbfounded as I was to learn that Eddie Hinton isn't black.

Two Unsung Heroes

The southern states of America are strewn with great, neglected singers, and Kip Anderson and Tommy Tate number among the very greatest. Their voices were strikingly similar: rich, liquid-chocolate tenors which sounded simultaneously gravelly and deeply resonant. Kip's perhaps had a more rural inflection to it, a looser, more Lee Dorsey-ish warmth, but they both give one the same kind of pleasure – a timbre somewhere between the rounded baritonal power of James Carr and the piercing 'beautiful scream' of O. V. Wright.

Anderson only left a handful of sides behind when, to all intents and purposes, he disappeared from the domain of southern soul. The best were his woeful Muscle Shoals ballads 'Without a Woman' and 'Take It Like a Man', together with the funky 'A Knife and a Fork' and a couple of rather more primitive waxings – above all a rapturous version of Little Willie John's 'Letter from My Darling' – on Nashville's Excello label; there isn't much else. All of these performances are characterized by a multi-hued voice with an instinctively inventive sense of timing.

Tate's long and chequered career has encompassed stints as a singer, as a drummer, and as a songwriter, a role in which he currently makes a comfortable living at Malaco Records in his hometown Jackson, Mississippi. A sweet-natured, unassuming man with funny little mole-like eyes and a shy, half-stuttered way of speaking, Tommy could almost be a southern Luther Vandross, the difference being only that, where Vandross reared himself on Bacharach and Tamla Motown, Tommy was raised on gospel and blues. Both voices are so big, so *thick* – compare Tate's 'Listen to the Children' on his 1981 Juana album with early Luther – that they never need to scream.

Tommy singing on 1985's 'What Gives You the Right' doesn't sound markedly different from the Tommy of the '60s OKeh side 'A Lover's Reward', or for that matter from the phenomenally powerful voice on 'Just A Little Overcome' by the Nightingales, whose Ollie Hoskins he briefly replaced in 1971. Throughout his absurdly inauspicious twenty-five years in the business he has sung with consistent and majestic skill, even when it's just trotting out golden oldies in a bar: when I caught him singing in Jackson in 1985 he was doing everything from a scatted 'What's Goin' On' to a semi-stomped 'Knock on Wood'.

As Malaco's Tommy Couch said to me the next day, 'You and I know that Tommy Tate is one of the greatest singers in America, but . . .'

VII

Lady Soul

ARETHA AND THE SISTERS

'Each time I go to bed I pray like Aretha Franklin . . .'
SCRITTI POLITTI

If many of the female singers spawned by the black gospel world were heavily built earth mamas with booming alto and contralto voices, there was another kind of singer – more diva than matriarch, more angel than empress – whose higher-pitched, usually soprano, voice paved the way for a similar archetype, the '60s Soul Sister. Marion Williams may have dominated the Clara Ward Singers in their '50s heyday, but it was Ward herself, with her high, almost nasal alto, who proved the major influence on the young Aretha Franklin.

Aretha fell under Clara's particular spell when that glamorous, hard-headed woman became a regular companion to her father the Rev C. L. Franklin, the hugely popular pastor of the New Bethel Baptist Church in Detroit. Aretha's mother, Barbara Siggers, is always supposed to have had a strong voice, but she deserted her husband and five children when Aretha was just six years old, after which the withdrawn, unhappy girl found a series of surrogate mothers in gospel matriarchs like Mahalia Jackson and Marion Williams. Nobody got closer to her, or took more time with her, than Clara, and fittingly it was Clara's most famous hymns – 'Precious Lord', 'The Day Is Past and Gone', and others – that Aretha sang as a fourteen-year-old prodigy in her father's church.

'The voice is no longer so high, but it remains freakishly resonant,' Tony Heilbut wrote of Clara Ward in 1971. 'Her nasality, almost Middle Eastern in its penetration, makes her a peerless moaner, and her solo records of the hymns . . . were so brilliant in phrasing and so compelling in spirit that she out-ranked Mahalia Jackson in a newspaper poll.' It is a version of this voice, touchingly girlish and thin but really no less commanding than its original, which one hears in the recordings Joe Van Battle made of Aretha at the New Bethel Church in 1956. The tender voice intermittently cracks but all of Ward's signature effects are there, just as they are in the voices of *Amazing Grace* (1972) and *One Faith, One Lord, One Baptism* (1987): the moans and slides, the breathtaking sustain, the enunciation of words like 'Jesus' ('Jeheesus'). And when she moans, wrote Gerri Hirshey, 'the motherless child sounds like mother to all'.

It's a voice of dazzling virtuosity from the start, then – a virtuosity almost disturbing in one so young. As with any very precocious talent, there is an implicit discrepancy between the singer's immaturity and the emotional reach of the voice, as if a child had no right to sound so *ancient* with gospel's woes. But then, rather like Michael Jackson, perhaps Aretha Franklin never really had a childhood. And perhaps her emotional life has always been subsumed by her art, which would explain why so many of her recorded performances have a curious coldness about them.

The pure sound of the voice is not that remarkable or even 'moving'; on certain ballads – the version of Johnny Ace's 'Never Let Me Go' is a good example – the timbre is almost anodyne, blanched, and certainly not that of a gospel earth mama. Everything is in the assurance and the high-wire swoops of her phrasing, 'the way she carries herself', and to watch her on film is to see someone whose whole body and psyche are completely concentrated in the act of singing. This is the whole of her being, and yet – paradoxically – to listen to her is rarely an intimate experience, for little is revealed or exposed by this frightened, agoraphobic woman whose art is somehow so bound up within herself.

Aretha is always soaring away, as if trying to lose herself. In Wilfred Mellers's characteristically quaint phrase, 'the quasi-superhuman *sostenuto* of her line wafts her among the angels'. If, purely as a singer, she has not been that influential, it is simply because no one has been able to 'keep up' with her. Her lines tend to be clean and straight rather than arabesque or melismatic, and what stand out more than anything are the sudden, high, almost indignant phrases you hear on classic Atlantic hits like 'I Never Loved a Man' and 'Doctor Feelgood': the 'how could you' and 'baby you know' of 'I Never Loved a Man', the whooping 'yeah's and 'you's at the end of 'Doctor Feelgood'. The mercurial intelligence of her timing, her compression of phrases within the minutest gaps, is astonishing, and yet it is this intelligence which – running rings round us as it does – can so often lose us.

Compare Aretha's version of 'Dark End of the Street' with the various male versions of the song, and notice the way hers loses all the song's sombre, doomed power. There is no build here, just a relentless, full-throttle display of skills and tricks, something Russell Gersten observed in her reading of Bobby

Bland's 'Share Your Love with Me': 'She rips the whole thing apart, slurring over key lines and emphasizing the syllables one would least expect. Her attitude is that no mere lyricist is going to tell *her* what the song is about.' Peter Guralnick puts it with admirable restraint – 'there have been occasions when she has done little more than show off the purely technical aspects of her voice, treating songs more as vocal exercises than as opportunities for emotional engagement' – but I would have to agree with Tony Heilbut's verdict that many of her (soul) performances have been 'tired, melodramatic, and extravagant'. Even Jerry Wexler, who rescued her after six ignominious years of MOR jazz-pop on Columbia, has found her culpable for 'oversouling'.

It is odd that the 'Queen of Soul' should have taken such a long and inappropriate diversion to get from gospel back to gospel-based R&B – and delightfully ironic that Columbia should have called one of her albums *Soul Sister* (1965) – but as with so many icons of 'soul' (Ray Charles, Sam Cooke, for examples) her musical style is actually made up of several anomalous strands. 'They used to call me a jazz singer,' she told Val Wilmer in 1968. 'Now I think what I sing is closer to R&B and straight blues, sometimes a little pop mixed with blues . . .' If Columbia drove themselves mad trying to turn her into a black Barbra Streisand – listen to Mahalia Jackson fighting it out with Nancy Wilson on Aretha's 1961 version of 'It Ain't Necessarily So' – it was Franklin herself who insisted on cutting 'Over the Rainbow' on her very first LP for the label, and who reverted back to pop in the '70s with her versions of 'Let It Be', 'Eleanor Rigby', and 'Bridge Over Troubled Water'. Indeed, some of her loveliest performances – the 1968 version of Sam Cooke's 'You Send Me', the brilliant Quincy Jones arrangement of Bernstein and Sondheim's 'Somewhere' (1973) – have been with material only tangentially rooted in gospel. If the Aretha who sang 'Walk On By' on Columbia was straining to rein in her bluesy slurs and flattenings, the Atlantic artist who tackled another Dionne Warwick song, 'I Say a Little Prayer', had achieved a much happier balance between gospel-soul and jazz-pop.

Franklin is nonetheless at her best on the pared-down gospel-blues of 'Never Loved A Man', of 'Going Down Slow', and Willie Nelson's 'Night Life'; or alternatively – the flipside of the coin – on the southern country-soul of 'Do Right Woman – Do Right Man', where her voice stays in a cool, low register for almost the whole song. In these performances she is sufficiently grounded not to have to show off: in Russell Gersten's words, 'When she was on target, she worked on two levels simultaneously – blues reality, romantic fantasy; upfront sexuality, tacit vulnerability,' and it is this almost ambivalent interplay, one which epitomizes so much great singing, that you experience in her finest records.

It's worth noting, incidentally, how much work Aretha puts into a vocal performance, how carefully she thinks through every line of every song she records. 'When it comes to the ABCs of music I am no dummy,' she told Gerri Hirshey. 'I always worked on my sound, my arrangements, *before* I went into the studio with a producer.' Jerry Wexler recalls Franklin sitting at an electric piano with the Sweet Inspirations, 'lining out' a song's vocal arrangement, while Luther Vandross, who produced her best '80s album, *Jump To It*, says she'd done her homework so thoroughly on it that she sang the astonishing title track – with all its scat passages, erotic exclamations, Luther-esque shudders, and dizzying octave jumps – in a single take. 'She swept into the studio in a track suit with a fur coat over it, did her vocal, and swept out again,' he laughs. 'It was like: "Who *was* that masked woman?!?" '

The Aretha of the '80s and '90s – of guest cameos and superstar duets – sounds airier, huskier, more matronly than the Lady Soul of 'Respect' and 'Natural Woman'. On 'Sweet Bitter Love' (1985), she is even close to taking off Gladys Knight, the original singer of the song. If she is still doing Clara Ward songs – 'Jesus Hears Every Prayer' and 'Surely God Is Able' on her second gospel comeback album *One Faith, One Lord, One Baptism* – she is taking it easier vocally, a dowager duchess rather than a reigning monarch. For the most part I remain curiously untouched by her, even a little numbed by the bravura technique. But I doubt that I will ever find her less than fascinating.

Sisters

If there are few soul sopranos who've been able to 'keep up' with the queen, there are a small handful – Tommie Young, Shirley 'Woman to Woman' Brown, the gospel singer Vanessa Bell Armstrong come to mind – who have come within her range. Occasionally, too, they've packed the emotional punch Aretha has lacked: listen to Brown's pinched, lacerating wail in the melismatic passages of 'It Ain't No Fun' (1974), or to the besotted, tumbling devotion of Armstrong's 'Peace Be Still' (1983), for some spine-chilling singing. At the other end of the Franklin spectrum, Dionne Warwick sang her Bacharach/David masterpieces in a voice whose timbre, despite her apprenticeship with New Jersey's Drinkard Singers, was about as far as you could get from black gospel: a white, gossamer-thin soprano which remains an acquired taste, however perfect her impeccably economical phrasing was for 'Walk On By' or 'Anyone Who Had a Heart'.

One of the truly great *divas* of uptown soul was Linda Jones, whose death from a diabetic attack in 1972 robbed the world of a freakishly distinctive soprano voice. This is the polar opposite of the earth mama larynx, a chalkily hard, brittle sound which frequently threatens to splinter and yet mesmerizes through its hysterical intensity. Dave Godin found it 'in the nicest possible way strangely disturbing', and one knows what he meant. Her way of bearing down on the short 'o' vowel, cramming every available space with melismatic 'woah-ooo-oh's, conveyed a kind of manic frustration, as though she could never impress her love strongly enough: constantly she strives to push the point home, heaping – on 'Give My Love a Try', for instance – beleaguered assurance upon beleaguered assurance.

Jones's other great trademark is the high falsetto cry she whips out when she can't climb any higher in her natural range, a sort of strangulated yell which reaches its all-time climax in the cataclysmic rendition of 'For Your Precious Love' recorded not very long before her death. Russell Gersten observed that singing had become a 'life and death matter' for Jones during her last sessions, and certainly this last testament of delirious desolation has something frighteningly urgent about it: even the sermonette intro, borrowed from Oscar Toney's version, is delivered at breakneck speed. As for the shuddering, apparently uncontrollable cries that lift one from peak to further peak – as Robert Christgau noted, the record starts with a climax and builds from there – by the end they are virtually unbearable. Never has so much been wrung out of such a frequently covered song.

Kicking off her career with sub-Motown dance sides in the early '60s – the kind worshipped by Northern Soul devotees in the '70s – Jones is supposed to have been very influenced by that slick, sobbing soulman Jackie Wilson, and even recorded a version of his 'Lonely Teardrops' in 1963. If it is true, she was a good deal less fluid, less trilling, than Wilson, and her voice only came into its own on ballads like 'The Things I've Been Through' (1967) or more Philly-esque records like 'I'll be Sweeter Tomorrow' (1969), songs which gave her breathless delivery the kind of space it needed. By the time of her last single, 'Not On the Outside', she was taking the soul voice to places it had never been before and all but choking on the frenzied effort it was costing her.

Losers Weepers

There was a kind of Soul Sister, too, who excelled at playing the victim and rarely hollered for the 'Respect' Aretha demanded. Her domain was balladry of an almost abject variety, three-minute vinyl versions of the Hollywood 'weepie' in which the voice was always close to tears: not for Bettye Swann or Loleatta Holloway the vengeful huffing of the earth mama.

No more fragile purity exists in all the recorded pain of womankind than in the voice of Bettye Swann, a trembling country-nasal soprano that nestles in your neck with no hint of reproach or revenge. This is the least hammy of broken-hearted nymphs, suffering what Simone Weil called 'affliction', when the spirit is bewildered and numb. Everything here is in the timbre, so nasal it sounds as if she has a cold, and in the superbly restrained vibrato. Bettye never tries to dazzle, always holding back and implying: her reading of 'I'd Rather Go Blind', for example, is coy and secretive next to Etta James's brooding, while the 'crying time' of 'Today I Started Loving You Again' (a Merle Haggard song highly susceptible to soul treatment) is a matter more of relief than of anguish. If she sounded lovely on her 1965 hit 'Make Me Yours' and her Joe Simon-style country adaptations on Capitol, her masterpieces – above all 'I'm Just Living a Lie' and 'Be Strong Enough to Hold On' – date from her early '70s period in Muscle Shoals. 'Every time you take her in your arms/I feel your touch all over me again', she warbles on 'Living a Lie', and it's impossible not to feast on such muted masochism.

More famous now as the frantic voice of the 1989 Black Box dancefloor hit 'Ride On Time', Loleatta Holloway was actually one of the great weepers of '70s soul, as evidenced by the ecstatically tortured Sam Dees song 'Cry to Me'. (Nor, by all accounts, did she balk at weeping openly when it came time to protest Black Box's unacknowledged sampling of her howls.) Another magnificent Dees song, 'Worn Out Broken Heart', almost topped 'Cry to Me', and if Loleatta was never as distinctive or subtle a singer as Bettye Swann, she had her moments of lachrymose splendour. Sam Dees seems almost to have cornered the 'weepie' market in the mid-'70s: one of the better songs which that tremulous-sounding *chanteuse* Margie Joseph – a more urbane Bettye Swann – recorded was Dees's 'Just As Soon As the Feeling's Over' (1975). More affectingly plaintive than Margie were Dorothy Moore, whose classic country-soul hit 'Misty Blue' was the perfect vehicle for her pleading, limpid style, and Ella Washington, a sharp soprano equally at home in the throes of heartache and ecstasy but at her sensuous best on the dreamy country song 'He Called Me Baby'. 'It was good to me,' born-again Ella later said of her soul years, 'but it was all "my baby left me" and "another man's wife" . . .' A fitting epitaph, perhaps, for the weeping losers of southern soul.

The most extraordinary female singer to emerge in Aretha Franklin's wake in the '70s was never a Soul Sister *per se*, but she *was* born in Georgia, and a pronounced deep soul timbre, slightly reminiscent of Barbara Lynn, was an essential ingredient in her supernaturally elastic voice. The world first heard Randy Crawford on the Crusaders' 'Street Life' (1979), but she'd made her début four years earlier with a live recording of 'Everything Must Change' at LA's Shrine Auditorium, a performance which still ranks among her greatest. Here, in embryo, is everything that astonishes one in 'One Day I'll Fly Away', in 'You Might Need Somebody', in the awesome 1979 version of Jerry Butler's 'I Stand Accused': the fluttering vibrato and curiously taut melisma; the flipping from hushed, little-girlish intimacy to defiant wailing; the wide, ringing resonance on long 'i' vowels (as in 'fly', 'right', 'life'); and the general sensation of sound coming from places one didn't know existed.

In the previously uncharted borderlands between deep soul and MOR-jazz, Crawford does things with lungs, larynx, breath, and natural human amplification that no one has ever done before. Like a great athlete, and like Aretha Franklin – with whom, interestingly, she has a certain paranoid reclusiveness in common – she is a glorious freak of nature.

VIII

Uptown

THE URBAN SOUL MEN

If the preachers and balladeers of southern country-soul had the most harrowing, haunting black voices of all, the rather more dapper gentlemen of the big northern cities – in particular Chicago, Detroit, New York, and Philadelphia – boasted their fair share of exceptional singers, men who for the most part cried or testified in an altogether more *refined* manner than their Memphis counterparts but whose voices afford one no less pleasure for that. Tamla Motown may have processed soul in exactly the same way some American blacks 'processed' their hair – contorting it into Caucasian shapes, forcing its natural patterns into straight lines – but its greatest records hinged on the blending of super-sophisticated production with raw gospel voices. Playing the Copacabana didn't stop the Temptations' David Ruffin and Eddie Kendricks, both southern-born and church-reared, from tearing up the house Swan Silvertones-style.

It was Charlie Gillett, in his definitive *Sound of the City*, who first used the term 'uptown' to denote the artfully arranged and often lushly orchestrated pop-soul fashioned by producers as diverse as Bert Berns in New York, Carl Davis in Chicago, and Smokey Robinson in Detroit. 'Uptown' was everything southern soul wasn't: sweet, smooth, and eclectic enough to use not only strings and choirs but vibes, French horns, even glockenspiel. By the time uptown soul reached its symphonic apex in the '70s, with Thom Bell's and Van McCoy's gloriously saccharine productions for the Stylistics, you couldn't have got much further away from the music's gospel roots. 'Uptown' was where the ghetto met Brill Building pop, where singers like Jerry Butler, Garnet Mimms, and Chuck Jackson sang songs by Bacharach & David, Goffin & King, and Mann & Weil (authors of the Crystals' 'Uptown', no less). From New York records like Ray Pollard's 'The Drifter' to Hollywood productions like Phil Spector's masterworks of blue-eyed soul with the Righteous Brothers (which included not just the epic 'You've Lost That Lovin' Feeling' but also those staples of sob 'Ebb Tide' and 'Unchained Melody'), it was the sound of black soul in unholy union with white symphonic melodrama.

Uptown soul had its roots in the sobbers and doo-woppers of the '50s, in the voices of Clyde McPhatter, Jackie Wilson, Sam Cooke, and Roy Hamilton – all singers who crossed from R&B to pop and back so many times that they blurred the boundaries between them. The interconnections were manifold: Berry Gordy, who in Tamla Motown was to found an uptown soul empire, wrote two of Jackie Wilson's biggest hits, 'Reet Petite' and 'Lonely Teardrops', while Garnet Mimms's mentor Bert Berns had worked – alongside Leiber & Stoller, Burt Bacharach, Phil Spector, and numerous other architects of uptown soul – with the Drifters at Atlantic. It was Berns, reflecting the 'melting pot' ambience of New York, who introduced the Latin American *baion* rhythm into R&B, a rhythm which spread all the way from the Drifters' great hits to the classic songs – like 'He Will Break Your Heart' – that Curtis Mayfield wrote for Jerry Butler in Chicago.

Jerry Butler was arguably the first uptown soulman. Joe McEwen sees 'For Your Precious Love', that timeless ballad Butler wrote and sang as front man in the original Impressions, as 'the first soul record', by which he means the first vocal group record of the '50s to serve purely as a vehicle for a solo gospel voice, in this case a rich, devotional baritone barely offset by Curtis Mayfield's weird tenor and the group's other voices. Months before Ben E. King first stood out as a distinctive baritone 'soul' voice in the Drifters (on that primal New York 'beat concerto' 'There Goes My Baby'), Butler, who'd sung with Mayfield in the Northern Jubilee Gospel Singers, was turning the conventions of doo-wop inside out and singing as an uptown balladeer.

It was a beautiful, restrained performance, though one that Jerry only managed to follow up after he'd detached himself from the Impressions and spent two years out in the cold. Ironically, it was Mayfield, yet to prove himself as the Impressions' new leader, who came to his rescue, providing him with a feast of hits that reflected the uptown pop influence of New York: besides 'He Will Break Your Heart' they included 'Find Another Girl', 'I'm a Telling You', and 'Need to Belong', all of them imprinted with Mayfield's cool, delicate touch and mercurial guitar fills. Like the best Brill Building songs, this was inner-city folk music, but with a subtle Chicago twist.

It wasn't long before Butler was singing New York songs like the Bacharach/David classics 'Make It Easy On Yourself' and 'Message to Martha' and the Van McCoy number 'I Can't Stand to See You Cry'. He even scored with the first pop version of 'Moon River', earning the gratitude of Henry Mancini and

Johnny Mercer for helping to make it 1961's Song of the Year. 'Make It Easy' must be his all-time greatest performance, the perfect platform for this huge, ruby-warm voice with its elegant, velvety vibrato and almost operatic phrasing. There is a weary, defeated groan in the last bars of the song which must count as one of the saddest sounds ever emitted by a human being; unlike, say, Chuck Jackson in New York, Jerry has a 'grain' of awkward, bashful vulnerability in his voice that creates real pathos. When I saw the Impressions' 1983 reunion show at Los Angeles's Greek Theatre, he groaned exactly as he does on the record, then shuffled back into the darkness with the words 'It makes you wanna cry'. It was almost unbearably moving.

When Chicago's uptown sound started to fade towards the end of the '60s, Butler's new label Mercury took the sensible precaution of packing him off to the new mecca of uptown soul Philadelphia, whose leading lights Gamble & Huff had formulated a sound at once more up-tempo and more intricately orchestrated than anything heard in Chicago, or in Detroit and New York come to that. Butler's year of Philly hits – including 'Never Give You Up', 'Hey Western Union Man', and the Top 5 'Only the Strong Survive' – put the city firmly on the soul map and gave his voice a new setting, one that required less torchy resonance and more Soul Man *chutzpah*. (Even Wilson Pickett came down for the Gamble & Huff treatment – as did that Butler-soundalike Joe Simon.) Philly DJ Georgie Woods dubbed Butler the Iceman, because of his ice-cool delivery, and the nickname showed how far he'd come from the warmth of his Vee Jay days. Like Chuck Jackson he ended up on Motown, by now a bastion of ritzy, uptown values, and recorded a series of nondescript, hit-free albums for them through the latter half of the '70s.

Walter Jackson was a more idiosyncratic version of Jerry

Butler, a Detroit native whose thoughtful, almost conversational baritone took the Butler sound, replete with all the little groans and sighs, into the realm of supper-club easy-listening. Indeed, despite having two of his great OKeh sides written and produced for him by Curtis Mayfield, Jackson thought of himself primarily as a pop and MOR singer, and crooned 'My Funny Valentine' and 'Moonlight in Vermont' alongside 'It's All Over' (1964), 'It's an Uphill Climb (From the Bottom)' (1966), and the haunting 'Speak Her Name' (1967). It remains an extraordinarily compelling voice, one which always resists the baritonal tendency to over-dramatize. Even on the rather schlocky Bacharach song 'They Don't Give Medals (To Yesterday's Heroes)', the phrasing has an engaging uncertainty about it, while 'Speak Her Name' almost anticipates that off-beat gypsy soulboy Tim Buckley. In the mid-'70s, he teamed up with his old OKeh mentor Carl Davis for the first of four albums on Davis's Chi-Sound label, all of which dispensed with any pretensions to R&B and plumped for a mixture of MOR–pop covers with revisitings of OKeh hits like 'Welcome Home', 'What Would You Do' and 'It's All Over' – all sung very soulfully, of course, in a voice that had deepened and mellowed yet further with time. A polio victim from childhood, Jackson died tragically of a stroke in 1983.

New York-based baritones like Chuck Jackson and Tommy Hunt sounded even more 'uptown' than Jerry Butler. If Jackson periodically showed that he was capable – on the William Bell song 'Any Other Way', for instance – of screaming in a voice that prefigured James Carr of all people, his staple vocal style seemed to derive as much from jazz balladeers Billy Eckstine and Arthur Prysock, with their deep, leathery vibratos, as from Ben E. King or Nappy Brown. This is not altogether surprising, given that he was Scepter's male version of Dionne Warwick and the fortunate recipient of such Burt Bacharach gems as 'Any Day Now', 'I Just Don't Know What to Do with Myself', and – with its pizzicato string passage – 'I Wake Up Crying'. This was Brill Building soul at its classiest, with Carole King arranging 'I Don't Want to Cry' (1961) and Leiber and Stoller producing him on such radically bizarre 'beat concertos' as 'I Keep Forgettin'' and 'Millionaire' (both 1962), and if the singing generally is too mannered and artful to touch one deeply, on something like his version of that white vocal group classic 'Since I Don't Have You' his melisma is agile and supple enough to suggest a baritonal Jackie Wilson.

Labelmate Tommy Hunt, a graduate like Jackson of the East Coast vocal group sound – he was in the Flamingoes where Chuck was in the Del-Vikings – cut at least one early uptown classic in 'Human' (1961), as well as 'I Just Don't Know What to Do' and another Bacharach/David chestnut 'Don't Make Me Over'. Always overshadowed by Jackson, who often shared the same Scepter backing tracks, his baritone was never different enough to stand out in the symphonic soul stakes. A superior male outlet for Bacharach and David's uptown pop-soul songs, though he never had a hit like 'Human', was Lou Johnson, whose subtle reworkings of the Dionne Warwick classics (particularly 'Always Something There to Remind Me') were sung in a low tenor voice that, like Solomon Burke's, combined polished, nightclubby phrasing with a raw timbre, in his case one that recalls the frantic sound of Spencer Wiggins.

Bert Berns had already helped to establish Solomon Burke and Ben E. King as 'Soul' singers (if not 'Soul' men) when Garnet Mimms and the Enchanters wound their way up to New York from Philadelphia in 1962. But where Burke and King were as much honorary southerners as 'uptown' singers, Mimms's high, superbly modulated tenor was at the other end of the spectrum, the ideal vehicle for Berns's symphonic soul vision. It was a voice that came almost directly out of the sobbing McPhatter–Wilson line, though usually refraining from the wanton hysteria of Clyde and Jackie: if 'Don't Change Your Heart' (1963) suggested the operatic delirium of the Dominoes, the Joe Tex-ish 'That Goes to Show You' (1965) was as finely controlled as a Sam Cooke ballad.

As with Jerry Butler and the Impressions, Garnet Mimms and the Enchanters – who'd grown out of the Gainors back in Philly – were hardly a vocal group in the '50s street-corner sense of the term: more a showcase for Mimms's solo voice. In any case, for the most part Bert Berns preferred to use the likes of Cissy Houston and Dionne and Dee Dee Warwick as backing singers on Garnet's classic sides, creating a kind of uptown gospel choir for the gushing choruses of 'Cry Baby' and 'Baby Don't You Weep'. Lifted by these exceptional voices, Mimms positively sailed through the Berns–Ragovoy songbook, from 'Cry Baby' (1963) through the mighty 'It Was Easier to Hurt Her' (1965) to 'I'll Take Good Care of You' (1966), his biggest hit after the inevitable breakaway as a solo artist. His was an adaptable voice, too, as much at home in Solomon Burke-style material like 'More Than a Miracle' and Brook Benton's 'It's Just a Matter of Time', or Drifters-style *baion* ballads like 'A Quiet Place' (a song about getting out of the city), as in Jerry Ragovoy barn-stormers like 'My Baby'. His finest moment, though, was the rapturous 1963 version of 'For Your Precious Love', which faithfully followed Jerry Butler's vocal line but trounced the original in its heart-stopping interplay between Mimms and his backing singers.

Jerry Ragovoy, who continued to record Mimms for Verve after United Artists dropped the singer in 1967, was the man responsible for another remarkable voice, the wildly wailing tenor of Howard Tate, who'd sung with Mimms in the Gainors. Tate was Ragovoy's revenge against southern soul, an 'uptown' singer who could sing blues songs like 'Part-time Love' and 'How Blue Can I Get?', or deep soul ballads like 'Get It While You Can' and 'I Learned It All the Hard Way', and do it as well as anyone below the Mason–Dixon line. Both Ragovoy and Bert Berns had been forced to respond to the emergence of southern soul, with its raw emotion and simple 'head' arrangements. Berns, while concentrating equally on the pop acts signed to his Bang label (the McCoys, Neil Diamond, Them), formed Shout to record singers like Freddie Scott, another excellent baritone whose sides included a seminal version of 'Cry to Me', and Aretha Franklin's sister Erma, with her classic 'Piece of My Heart'. Ragovoy, meanwhile, wrote and produced Lorraine Ellison's shattering 'Stay With Me', a high-watermark of uptown soul balladry, and began collaborating with Doc Pomus's erstwhile partner Mort Shuman, one of the Brill Building veterans.

With Shuman, Ragovoy wrote two of the songs – including the title track, subsequently cut by Janis Joplin – that made up Howard Tate's great 1967 album *Get It While You Can*. Tate's high, shrieking tenor, breaking at regular intervals into a unique falsetto, was closer to southern wailers like Jimmy Hughes and Roscoe Shelton than it was to the dreamy uptown voice of Garnet Mimms. On 'Part-time Love' he could be a fuller, richer Johnnie Taylor, his bitterly bluesy tone offset by fluent melismatic skills. A 1972 album for Atlantic, with Ragovoy still at the helm, forsakes the soul discipline of the Verve period, venturing into pseudo-funk and rock covers which don't really work. Much better is a solitary Epic side, 'Ain't Got Nobody to Give It To', produced by Ragovoy in 1974.

In Detroit, as in New York and Chicago, a pop-R&B fusion emerged before 'soul' as such ever came into being. The first release on Berry Gordy's Tamla label, Marv Johnson's 'Come to Me' (1959), was very much in the vein of the songs Gordy had written for Jackie Wilson – in the words of Joe McEwen and Jim Miller, 'a clean R&B record that sounded as white as it did black', with Johnson's falsetto wailing over a jaunty up-tempo track powered by a pop-doowop bass singer. As the Motown sound developed, though, it found an uptown identity all its own, one that for all its meticulously choreographed vaudeville razzle was younger and more dance-oriented than the uptown soul produced in New York and Chicago. This was the 'brand new beat' of Martha Reeves and the Vandellas' 'Dancing in the Street', a trebly, propulsive sound in which the lead voice was often just another detail, rather than a central feature, in the total picture of the production. One need only compare Diana Ross, Motown's reigning queen through the '60s, with Aretha Franklin, to see that vocal power was not necessarily central to the Motown sound. Indeed, it was only when Berry Gordy saw the threat which the new soul sisters posed to his girl-group sound that Gladys Knight, a magnificently husky singer who already had a track record behind her, was signed to a Motown subsidiary called, simply and fittingly, Soul.

There were some great singers on Motown, of whom one (Knight) has already been discussed and another (Smokey Robinson) is being saved for the following chapter. The best were rasping baritones like Levi Stubbs of the Four Tops and David Ruffin of the Temptations – Motown's very own Redding and Pickett – whose inelegant, painfully ragged voices were far removed from the massaging larynxes of Jerry Butler or Chuck Jackson. If Stubbs began 'Baby I Need Your Loving' (1964) or 'Ask the Lonely' (1965) in a voice almost Butler-mellow, by the end of both he was barking like a wild dog, a sound which was never pretty or subtle at the best of times but which Holland

Dozier & Holland, dragging it from his throat with little consideration for his long-term career, used to splendid effect on the Tops' classic sides. The trouble, of course, is that Stubbs is always pushing and straining, throwing out his voice without the necessary support: even the mighty 'Reach Out' is, as it were, *hurled* at the listener with a guttural, almost a-musical breathlessness.

Ruffin, who was actually a low tenor, was prone to the same faults but was much less limited. His hard, frayed, muscular tone and nasal resonance was both more disciplined and more gospelly, capable of building from gentle verses to aggressive choruses, above all in the timeless songs – 'My Girl', 'It's Growing' and co. – written and produced for the Temps by Smokey Robinson. Under Norman Whitfield's direction, on the likes of 'Ain't Too Proud to Beg' and '(I Know) I'm Losing You', he was less subtle, though still offset by Eddie Kendricks's bittersweet falsetto. Going solo was perhaps a mistake, since Ruffin, with his stringbean physique and Buddy Holly glasses, never again enjoyed the quality of material he'd been used to with the Temps. Perhaps he should have gone back south – he'd once sung in the Dixie Nightingales with Ollie Hoskins – and recorded his version of 'If Loving You Is Wrong' in the proper surroundings. Rolling with soul's eddies and currents, he cut Harold Melvin and the Blue Notes' Philly classic 'I Miss You' – ironical given his transparent influence on Theodore Pendergrass Jr – then went uptown proper with the Van McCoy-produced *Who I Am* album in 1975. With its proto-disco Steve Gadd drum pattern and hyper-orchestral, Pearl & Dean-style arrangement, the top ten single 'Walk Away from Love' was way over the top as a piece of soul music but did boast – decimating falsetto flights and all – one of the great vocal performances of our time.

Dennis Edwards, Ruffin's replacement in the Temptations, had a stronger, purer scream than his predecessor: almost a *beautiful* scream, to be sure. It was the perfect voice for Norman Whitfield's mildly ludicrous psychedelic ghetto epics, a mixture of Johnnie Taylor at his harshest and Gladys Knight in her best belting mode, and gave us one of the all-time great soul screams coming out of the first harmonica passage in 'Ball of Confusion'. It's Edwards, of course, leading that haunting masterwork of '70s urban soul 'Papa Was a Rolling Stone', and the man still sounds fabulous on the sultry Sam Dees ballad 'You're My Aphrodisiac' (1984).

When the production team of Holland Dozier & Holland defected from the Motown camp in 1968 and set up their own Invictus label, they signed a group, the Chairmen of the Board, who were fronted by a bizarre and altogether more interesting version of Levi Stubbs. General Norman Johnson had already distinguished himself on the Showmen's 1961 classic 'It Will Stand', singing in a voice that was equal parts Jackie Wilson and Ira Tucker, but on 'Give Me Just a Little More Time' and 'Dangling on a String' (both 1970) he sounded like Stubbs gone mad. It was the same barking, strangulated yelp of H-D-H chestnuts like 'I Can't Help Myself', but broken up by rolls, trills, hiccoughs, and a style of phrasing that made Jackie Wilson sound unaffected.

The Stubbs/Ruffin line was so influential that for a while – at least until the silk-spun falsetto voices of the '70s came along – hard baritone leads seemed to dominate northern vocal groups: the ultimate vindication of the Rev Julius Cheeks, perhaps. In Chicago, producer Bobby Miller and arranger Charles Stepney spotlighted the gritty, almost southern growl of Marvin Junior as lead singer of the doo-wop veterans the Dells, exactly as Motown had done with Stubbs and Ruffin and Gamble & Huff would do with Teddy Pendergrass. Junior even took the lead on the new, uptown-soul version of the group's 1956 doo-wop classic 'Oh What a Night', which had originally been sung by high tenor Johnny Funches. In Philadelphia, the O'Jays seamlessly blended Walter Williams's Dennis Edwards-ish baritone with Eddie Levert's plummy, slightly 'covered' tenor, while Harold Melvin and the Blue Notes virtually became a backdrop for the fearsome heavyweight voice of Marvin Junior's most faithful disciple Pendergrass. ('It's a bit strange,' said one Philly DJ quoted in Tony Cummings's book *The Sound of Philadelphia* in 1974, 'a group who've been into all that show tune and nightclub stuff coming on with such a heavy soul thing . . .')

Compare Pendergrass to the Marvin Junior of 'Open Up My Heart' and 'I Wish It Was Me You Loved', or even of the symphonic, Jimmy Webb-esque medley 'Love Is Blue'/'I Can Sing a Rainbow', and it's immediately clear where Teddy took his cue from: here is the same breathy beseeching, building to haughty, raging shouts, the same astonishing power making up for lack of agility. But Pendergrass, taking the hard baritone lead to its extreme, marks the style's culmination and finale. The clumsy attempts at melisma on the epic 'I Miss You' (1972) may sound like a killer bull practising the art of courtly love, but his mesmerizing preacher-rap at the end of 'Bad Luck' (1974) will never be topped as a thrilling peak of up-tempo baritone exhortation. Certainly as a solo artist Pendergrass never did anything like it again.

In Motown's high tenor range Marvin Gaye, like Otis Redding, has become such an icon of soul that people rarely ask themselves how good a singer he was. The answer is that he made the best possible use of limited resources, with a voice whose tone and timbre, far from being special, were quite thin and pinched. With early Marvin, everything is in his cool, casual timing, the easy control of the long phrases in Smokey's 'Ain't That Peculiar': even playing the debonair Soul Man – the 'Stubborn Kind of Fellow' – he manages to sound distanced and diffident. Interestingly, he never wanted to sing 'the hot stuff' in the first place and preferred listening to Sinatra, Streisand, and Eydie Gorme. Like Sam Cooke, he said, he wanted to 'prove that our kind of music and our kind of feeling could work in the context of pop ballads'. Two years after recording 'I Heard It Through the Grapevine' (1968), surely the most overrated soul single of all time, he all but abandoned his tenor voice to sing in a disembodied falsetto (of which more in the next chapter).

Billy Stewart, with whom Gaye had sung in a Washington, DC doo-wop group called the Rainbows, managed to incorporate his pronounced jazz leanings into the basic mid-'60s Chicago soul style, recording two albums of standards for Chess that yielded the huge hit version of 'Summertime' in 1966. Scatting and swooping in a voice at one moment jazzily slurred and the next whiningly doo-woppy, his playfully instinctual phrasing, 'word doubling', and Jackie Wilson-esque rolling of the letter 'r' made him one of '60s soul's most freakishly exciting vocal artists, as unpredictable on the more orthodox Windy City soul of 'I Do Love You' and 'Temptation 'Bout to Get Me' as on his highly eccentric readings of 'Over the Rainbow' and 'Moon River'.

Perhaps the greatest uptown soul singer of all was the man who took the Chicago sound into a new era with 1968's breezily chugging 'Can I Change My Mind'. Ironically, southern-born Tyrone Davis had none of the sophistication of the Motown artists, mumbling his words like the Mississippi farmboy he was, but he did have the most heavenly, dreamy voice, a shimmering, hovering instrument that floated with a kind of languid ease over the massed horns of his Dakar sides. As it happens, he started out idolizing Bobby 'Blue' Bland – and let's not forget that even Bobby went uptown on one of his biggest hits 'Call on Me' (1963) – and was groomed accordingly by Carl Davis, who insisted the very Bland-ish 'A Woman Needs to Be Loved' be Tyrone's first single, with 'Can I Change My Mind' on the B-side. When the latter unexpectedly took off on a Houston radio station, Tyrone's breathy, softly nasal style – a warm flame that dances at words and glides over chords with an almost gingerly grace – was set for life, and he followed up with a string of forgivably derivative songs, all either tenderly solicitous or ingratiatingly remorseful: 'Is It Something You've Got', 'Turn Back the Hands of Time', and 'There It Is' were three of the most successful.

Even jostling with up-tempo drums and brass he is magnificent, 'bobbing and weaving' through phrases with an airy, undulating charm. Words slide into each other, honey-gold runs over the crude rhythmic crevices of 'Turning Point' and 'There's Got to Be an Answer'. Tyrone won't shout or turn Bland-guttural at the end of a phrase: the floating sustain of his pleading 'pleeeeease' or 'tiiiiiiiime' is always intimate and warmly urging. Even better are mid-tempo songs like 'Don't Let It Be Too Late' and the hypnotic 'Wish It Was Me', with their wistful, whispered falsetto passages and tinglingly delicate timing.

In the late '70s, Davis's uptown soul became ultra-slick and plastic-rose seductive: the Inner City Love Man at work, struggling to stay afloat in the disco flood. But the phrasing was as endearingly down-home as ever – 'resist you' becomes 'rezish-yoo', 'felt' is 'feyert' – and the timbre just as beautiful, especially on the slow candlelight funk of 'Be with Me' and 'In the Mood', with their great pockets of space and little hair-trigger guitar fills. In the '80s, shunted from one independent label to another, he was just one of many remarkable singers who could find no secure home in black music, depressing proof that uptown soul had become so urbanized and dance-oriented that beautiful voices were now virtually expendable.

Freaks and Angels

THE GREAT FALSETTO SINGERS

Ever since the days when castrati first sang in the royal courts of Europe, men have used 'false' alto and soprano voices in their singing. But unlike the tenors and baritones of comic opera, soul singers – many of them already mentioned in this book – have frequently employed falsetto as a technique for heightening emotion, or simply as a mode of vocal 'play' and contrast. In gospel, in doo-wop, in deep soul, this extraordinary sound of a man singing like a woman has produced some of the most ecstatic music ever recorded.

The falsetto came down to soul through the gospel quartets, in which the entire range of the human voice, from *basso profundo* to soprano, was usually covered. R. H. Harris frequently floated up into 'head voice' with the Soul Stirrers, while in the Swan Silvertones the arching alto of Claude Jeter, far from being a mere harmonic ingredient, was one of the principal lead voices. In the secular vocal group era, too, falsetto was dominant, from Clyde McPhatter through to doo-wop groups both black and white. Trilling away like the birds after which so many of those groups were named, these falsetto leads sang with a dreamy, free-form innocence, angelically transcending the mundane tribulations of male desire and heartbreak.

A group which bridged the doo-wop era with the uptown 'symphonic soul' sound of the '60s was Little Anthony and the Imperials, whose singer Anthony Gourdine had an effeminate, almost camp voice capable of stratospheric, McPhatter-esque flights of melisma. On the group's evergreen 'Tears On My Pillow' (1958) he pouted in his best 'baby' style, influencing everyone from the Skyliners' Jimmy Beaumont to the Four Seasons' Frankie Valli, but on the run of '60s hits produced for DCP by Teddy Randazzo he wailed over strings and tympani with unbridled teen angst, keeping the high tenor–falsetto sob of Clyde and Jackie alive in a new, massively orchestrated context. If 'Goin' Out of My Head' (1964) and 'Hurt So Bad' (1965) start with a mincing softness – 'love' becomes 'lav', 'looking' is 'lucking' – both build to choruses of epic proportions as Anthony, with a tear-jerking catch in the throat on 'hurt' and 'head', erupts in hangdog juvenile agony. By 'I Miss You So' (late 1965), Randazzo had gone so far over the top that Gourdine was virtually being upstaged by the glissando of the strings, but it remains an exquisite voice, if more than a little anachronistic in today's soul climate.

Gourdine was a major influence on the young Smokey Robinson, who thought he was made when Berry Gordy leased the first Miracles side, 'Got a Job' (1958), to the same New York label the Imperials recorded for. As a falsetto singer, Smokey was never as camp or melodramatic as Little Anthony – there is always a boyish vulnerability, a tone of melancholy sincerity, in Robinson's quivering vibrato – but ultimately he followed Anthony's precedent through the '60s, and, like Marvin Gaye, abandoned the rather strained high tenor register of his early up-tempo performances. From the classical doo-wop of '(You Can) Depend on Me' (1960) onwards, it is an entrancing sound, a soft shower of a voice whose whole stance is diagonally opposed to the predatory desire of the macho soulman.

Smokey is an angel-fairy, serenading or lamenting with a courtly, ethereal tenderness. Each line, uncoiling, as David Morse once put it, 'from a breathy intimate whisper into a clear, bright, continuously intense verbal pressure', spins within itself and melts away like a wisp of smoke. If Sam Cooke was an influence on Robinson – and you can just make him out on 'The Man in You' (1964) – the honeyed sandpaper timbre of 'You Send Me' is quickly dissipated in the blissed-out cooing of 'Ooo Baby Baby', 'More Love', 'I'll Try Something New': 'I'll gather melodies from birdies that fly/And compose a toon for you . . .' Smokey never had the cocksure up-tempo poise of a Cooke, and finds the long, breathless lines of 'Shop Around' heavy going. He needs space to draw out words like 'me' and 'feel', 'lie' and 'wild', 'you' and 'choose' and 'confused'; space to swoon into his seraphic, beatific trances.

In the '70s, after he'd left the Miracles and become Motown's vice-president, Robinson reached his discreet peak as a singer – no landmark *What's Goin' On* or *Music of My Mind* for him, just a series of quiet albums and occasional hits, smoochy appeals like 'Baby Come Close' and 'Cruisin'' (that heavenly slow burn in the era of spurious disco 'heat'). The ensuing decade gave us 'Being with You' and (from *Warm Thoughts*) the achingly lovely 'What's in Your Life for Me'/'I Want to Be Your Love'. It gave us 'Gimme What You Want', 'And I Don't Love You', and 'Why Do Happy Memories Hurt So Bad?', all overlooked tracks on criminally overlooked albums, miniatures of ironic, tragico-mic pathos that resonate with a benign weariness. 'Set me free from love's desire', he warbles on 'I've Made Love To You A Thousand Times', and every little ring in the mucous membranes speaks of the yearning to fly free.

Marvin Gaye was another singer who wanted to fly, to leave his mortal self behind. Where Robinson was wistful, and Stevie Wonder manically overreaching, Marvin sang in a voice that, for all its libidinal subject matter, transcended sensuality. Gerri Hirshey was right to call the voice of *Let's Get It On* 'serpent-soft', since its erotic goading was coldly reptilian rather than warmly sexual, the ghost rather than the body of desire. On *What's Goin' On*, the coolness is more appropriate, more patient and serenely Mayfield-esque, but increasingly through the '70s his falsetto – the disembodied voice of a soul zen master – strives to bypass emotion, to lose itself in a diffuse whirl of funk. If 'Sexual Healing' is a *sexy* record it is a curiously clinical sexuality we are talking about. Not for Gaye the dreamy longing of Eddie Kendricks on 'Just My Imagination' (1971), the most famous performance by an equally limited if more classically doo-wop-rooted falsetto, and one who had his fair share of Smokey Robinson songs in the '60s.

Curtis Mayfield's falsetto was even more cerebral than Gaye's, though retaining a breathy kind of intimacy that Marvin forsook. With his short, quirky phrases, his voice was like a darting, semi-spoken flame, at once assured and inquisitive, and generally dispensed with the pleasures of melisma and vibrato. There is nothing of Smokey's sweet swooning in the classic Impressions sides, although 'I'm So Proud' is close in feel to something like 'Ooo Baby Baby' (itself a Chicago-influenced record), and a version of Johnny Ace's 'Never Let Me Go' showed that Curtis was capable of a more orthodox doo-wop style. With the militant solo albums of the '70s, the voice became more coolly didactic, more righteously ascetic, than ever. More pleasurable was the keening, freakishly high falsetto of Rondalis Tandy, whose Texan trio the Van Dykes – as their beautiful 1965 hit 'No Man Is An Island' attests – modelled themselves meticulously on the Impressions, and even cut their own, considerably more impassioned version of 'Never Let Me Go'.

Just as the Van Dykes were a rare example of a secular southern vocal group, so Rondalis Tandy was a rare example of a southern falsetto soul singer. In contrast to the gravelly Baptist tenors and baritones at Stax and Fame, southern falsettos like those of Tandy, Ted Taylor, Aaron Neville, and (later) Al Green were eerily beautiful aberrations – so much so, indeed, that the late Ted Taylor was obliged to take up kung fu to defend himself against those who cast snide aspersions on his virility.

As it happens, Taylor's voice sounded neither male nor female, just painfully, hysterically alienated. When Ted wails, gospel, blues, and doo-wop come together like some unholy fusion of R. H. Harris, Clyde McPhatter, and Little Willie John. 'He had a tenor that he could just play with,' said Ted of 'Pops' Harris, but there is nothing playful about his own slippery, squealing melisma, which must rate as one of soul's more hard-to-acquire tastes. The mode varied – gospel lamentation on 'You've Been Crying', crawling blues on 'Days Are Dark', dreamy doo-wop on 'Be Ever Wonderful' – but the falsetto stayed the same: if Taylor is a vocal archangel he is a fallen one, with a voice that chills and curdles the blood. (Two of his sides were 'I Got the Chills', from 1958, and 'I Feel a Chill', recorded a decade later.) From his apprenticeship with LA vocal group the Cadets, through OKeh sessions with Billy Sherrill in Nashville, right up to the feverish, paranoid funk of late '60s sides like 'Something Strange Is Going On' and 'Who's Doing It to Who?', Ted was out on a limb, singing as though he'd been castrated by the love of his life.

The crown prince of falsetto melisma, and one of soul's more extraordinary characters, is Aaron Neville of that one-band history of New Orleans rhythm'n'blues the Neville Brothers. As anyone who saw him warbling 'I Don't Know Much' with Linda Ronstadt back in 1989 will know, few experiences can be as disarming as hearing the voice of an angelic choirboy float out of his fearsome heavyweight frame. With tattooed biceps the size of hams and the face of a hardened jailbird, he hardly looks the part of a singer whose forte is turning songs like Nat King Cole's 'Mona Lisa' and Bob Dylan's 'With God On Our Side' into chillingly beautiful displays of falsetto acrobatics. If he is happy enough to groove along with the gumbo of voodoo funk and reggae his brothers purvey, his finest work is invariably the gossamer-delicate balladry he handles on his own, either on Neville Brothers albums or on all-too-rare solo projects like his 1985 collection of doo-wop chestnuts *Orchid in the Storm*.

Along with the unlikely influence of such yodelling 'singing cowboys' as Gene Autry and the Sons of the Pioneers, doo-wop exerted a fascination on the young Neville that endures to this day. 'I used to have a little doo-wop group in high school,' he told me, 'and we'd be in the bathroom singing Spaniels and Flamingoes tunes when we should have been in class. That *was* my class.' Styling himself on heroes like the Spaniels' Pookie Hudson ('Goodnight, Well It's Time to Go') and the Orioles' Sonny Til ('Crying in the Chapel'), he developed a vocal technique which over the years has made him a singers' singer to soul and pop musicians the world over – a falsetto whose fluid, florid vocal arabesques turn kitsch trinkets like 'Mona Lisa' and 'Arianne' into baroque hymns of longing. On the revisionist doo-wop of the Penguins' 'Earth Angel' or Harvey and the Moonglows' 'The Ten Commandments of Love', the voice flutters like a butterfly, then ripples like a violin. Once he's up there, soaring and tumbling, anything can happen.

Except for the timelessly lovely 'Tell It Like It Is' (1966), a song of amorous woe whose title synched conveniently with a contemporary catchphrase of black power rhetoric, Aaron's recordings as a Crescent City Soul Man – most of them produced for Minit by Allen Toussaint – failed to give his voice the space or scope it needed. Only in the '70s, with isolated sides like 'Hercules' and 'The Greatest Love', did he properly find his feet, consolidating his reputation on Neville Brothers albums and on 'I Love Her Too', the gorgeous, Jack Nitzsche-produced theme song from *Heart Beat*. (Hear it for one passage of double-tracked roulades – melismatic flourishes – as detailed and dovetailed as a sequence of team gymnastics, with Aaron winding in and out of himself like a rococo Al Green.)

Today the voice is more exotic and unearthly than ever, an instrument whose elasticity can only be compared to that of Jackie Wilson, another of Neville's idols. 'People say they wish they could tell me what my voice does to them,' he smiles, 'and I say I wish I could tell them what it does to *me* to be able to sing like this.' At the time of writing, with the huge success of the Linda Ronstadt duets behind him, he is scheduled to record a solo album for A&M, a long-overdue reward for thirty years of dues-paying. If the Nevilles today are more renowned for their pan-Afro-American funk anthems than for their gauzy, diaphanous ballads, for a certain section of their cult following it will always be brother Aaron's turn in the spotlight that keeps one coming back.

For many people, the single greatest practitioner of the art of soul falsetto is that unlikely '70s superstar Al Green, whose 'head' voice was just one of several he had at his command. Identified by Tony Heilbut as 'a limber falsetto, a breathless crooner, and a growling preacher', and by Robert Christgau more cryptically as 'downhome, ersatz formal, and cute', these voices operate virtually as separate personalities, multi-tracked alter egos played off against each other in an intricate, intoxicating web of sound. Val Wilmer called him 'the most sensual singer on record', but he is more than that: he is the jester of soul, a meta-singer, a cat narcissistically chasing its own tail. No one has ever 'played' with the tones and textures of the human voice, or redefined the 'rules' of soul singing, like Al.

Green was an anomaly, an uneasy and febrile blend of uptown and down-home, from the start. Born and raised near Memphis in Arkansas, he moved at thirteen to Grand Rapids, Michigan, only to be thrown out of the family gospel group for listening to Jackie Wilson. In Grand Rapids he joined the local Creations and began emulating the Detroit–Chicago soulmen of the day: this is the voice you hear on pre-Hi sides like 'Back Up Train' and 'Hot Wire', urban soul records with funky arrangements and foxy female backing vocals released under the name 'Al Greene and the Soul Mates'. Here Al is playing the uptown soul brother of the late '60s, for the most part keeping his voice in a low tenor register as he huffs and puffs his way through the routine and derivative songs.

When Willie Mitchell heard him on a gig in Midland, Texas in 1970, the veteran trumpeter and producer sensed that Green was trying to be something he wasn't, but told him that with a different approach he could be a star: 'I told him we had to tone him down and get his range up 'cause he was singin' too hard.' Exactly what would have happened to Al Green without that fateful encounter is anyone's guess: what would he have been without Mitchell's brilliantly sparse, boxed-in sound? With it, he had all the time and space in the world to find his voice(s), which now seemed to draw, consciously or unconsciously, on the restraint and control of Claude Jeter's sweet falsetto hum, although fashioning it into something altogether more perverse and priapic.

Green is always two inches from your ear, reverb-free and nakedly self-absorbed. On long, slow-building songs like 'For the Good Times' and 'I Didn't Know', you can feel him edging and flinching around the mike, stuttering through regret and disbelief and dropping into slurred, mumbled madness. It's a voice which doesn't know whether to laugh or cry, a voice of comical seriousness and pure, schizoid play, 'evincing delight in sound', as Clive Anderson put it, 'where intellect, the understanding of every possibility, is also instantly intuitive'. Flipping between the rich, exaggeratedly open timbre of his tenor voice and the soft squeals of his falsetto, he is constantly veering from tension to release, mock-indignation to ecstatic dissipation of self. Moreover, there are few bravura flights of melisma: instead he favours short phrases, singing sometimes as if he can hardly bear to touch his words and would rather dance round them, brush them with the barest caress. There is no rhetoric, no declamation: if it is true – and it should not be surprising – that he in fact spent countless hours on his vocal tracks, the end result always sounds as freshly improvised as a jazz performance, flowing where instinct takes him. And always there are the overdubbed, parallel voices, nudging, prodding, commentating, played off against each other like reflections in a hall of mirrors.

Al Green pushes gospel fervour over the brink of credibility – or, as he puts it in his own inimitably mad way, 'music engulfs one's soul to exert himself (sic) beyond imagination'. This sense of being engulfed, especially on slow, trancelike songs like 'Simply Beautiful' or 'Jesus Is Waiting', is almost unique to him. One only has to see him onstage, lost in his natty little dance steps, kicking up his heels like some randy billy-goat, to feel that he is almost *possessed* by music. Few other singers could get away with singing unmiked as Green did in London to capacity crowds at the Albert Hall and Hammersmith Odeon: he succeeds because he is completely lost in the maddened joy of his singing. 'Strong as death, sweet as love/With the grace of a dove', he sang on a rare single from 1974, and he might have been describing his own dizzying, supernatural art.

There are few recorded voices as mesmerizingly freakish as Al Green's, but one of the more bizarre would have to be that of obscure deep-soul legend Roshell Anderson. Roshell's Excello sides 'Know What You're Doing When You Leave Me' and 'Snake Out of Green Grass' – both delightfully cheapo productions – showcase a voice whose deliberately flat notes and eccentric, almost recitative enunciation seem to be swallowed at the back of the throat: a plummy tenor ascending to whining head voice and taking a jazz singer's liberties with phrasing. For freakish falsetto virtuosity you'd be hard put to match the portly Detroit gospel singer Rance Allen, who recorded for Stax's Gospel Truth subsidiary in the '70s. With a big, resonant tenor that quickly gives way to high, raw shrieks, his shattering falsetto seems almost to dance and pirouette within itself, soaring over the instrumentation like a bird. 'God Is Wonderful' (1973) must rank as one of the most awesome falsetto performances ever recorded.

In the '70s, the falsetto lead mantle of Little Anthony and Smokey, of Curtis Mayfield and Eddie Kendricks, was inherited by the great Philly vocal groups – the Delfonics, the Stylistics, Blue Magic – together with the Chi-Lites in Chicago and the Moments in New York. To some extent these voices were interchangeable, stratospheric vehicles for the uptown-symphonic vision of producers like Thom Bell and Eugene Record. The arrangements were generally colossal (the Delfonics' 'Didn't I' is like Philly *à la* Phil Spector), the 'sweet soul' harmonies invariably diaphanous. But where William Hart's falsetto in the Delfonics was pinched and fragile, a plaintive variant on the Little Anthony blueprint, Russell Tompkins Jr in the Stylistics and Marshall Thompson in the Chi-Lites had syrupy, almost sickly voices that seem to epitomize one's memories of '70s soul at its naffest. If the Thom Bell/Linda Creed Stylistics ballads 'Betcha By Golly Wow' and 'You Make Me Feel Brand New' were divine, those Van McCoy-arranged hits 'I Can't Give You Anything' and 'Sixteen Bars' were grotesquely kitsch.

The two dominant black male stars of the '80s both employ falsetto more often than not. Neither Michael Jackson nor Prince are lauded very often as great *singers*, yet both do extraordinary things in this camply artificial register. Jackson was an uncannily artful singer even before his voice had broken, as one listen to the puckish dynamo of 'I Want You Back' – part Frankie Lymon, part kindergarten James Brown – makes clear. As pop's Peter Pan he compensates for the fundamental blandness of his timbre with an abundance of vocal tricks and games, most of them falsetto based. On the Jacksons' double live album from 1981 there is a remarkable half minute between 'I'll Be There' and 'Rock with You' that communicates more of Michael's sheer pleasure in singing than anything else he's ever done. Breaking free of accompaniment with the playful virtuosity of a saxophonist, he winds up 'I'll Be There' with a series of piercingly sustained shrieks, cutting up each one with a tiny, narcissistic chuckle. The audience goes predictably ape – reflex gratification – but for Jackson every breath, every laugh, every 'hick!', is a link, a phrase, a segment of the flow: so self-engrossed is he that his own responses are incorporated into the performance.

Jackson's is a voice of pure technique: it is scarcely black, let alone warm or sensual. (Even 'She's Out of My Life' – the last word in Sob! – sounds eerily inhuman.) Prince's falsetto is more sexual, more unashamedly camp. It is also more overtly styled on the great Philly falsettos, as is evidenced by the seraphic *a cappella* fanfare of his very first album; if Prince is first and foremost the psychedelic punk-funk merchant of, say, 'Let's Go Crazy', he is also the consummate erotic balladeer of 'Do Me, Baby', 'Condition of the Heart', and 'Adore', that swooning six-and-a-half-minute tribute to the uptown vocal group sound on *Sign O the Times*. His melisma here is superb, his tone simultaneously lewd and longing, and it is this Prince which will stay with me as a musical giant.

Ariel Swartley wrote of Prince that 'his falsetto literally confounds sexuality – it's a voice like a woman's coming from a man, but it's also a voice like a child's coming from an adult. Prince's home is in the midst of all the slippery indeterminacies falsetto implies'. The diminutive Minneapolitan sprite is only the latest in a long line of singers to have exploited such ambiguities for all they're worth.

X

White Heat

Van Morrison, Tim Buckley, Michael McDonald

It was Van Morrison who first made *me* want to sing. As an angst-ridden fifteen year old, weaned successively on glam, progressive, and West Coast rock, hearing his voice on *Astral Weeks* and *Moondance* for the first time was like connecting with a cry that had been latent inside me since puberty, a sound at once black and white, beautiful and barbaric, yearning and raging. Spike Milligan, chatting with Morrison in 1989 in a bizarre 'date' set up by *Q* magazine, talked of the sense of 'menace and abandonment' in his singing, and I can't think of two better words to describe the effect of this voice at its best.

Menace is certainly what one feels hearing Van Morrison on most of the recordings by Them, the Stones-ish R&B-pop group he fronted from late 1963 until mid-1966. It is little wonder that they were dubbed 'the Angry Young Them' when you hear the vicious voice of 'Gloria' or 'Baby, Please Don't Go' or 'Mystic Eyes', a 'beautiful snarl' which must rate as the most exciting punk-R&B voice of all time. 'He was small and gloomy,' wrote Greil Marcus, 'with more black energy than he knew what to do with.' On 'Bright Lights, Big City' he's a snot-nosed, mohair Howlin' Wolf, on 'Here Comes the Night' and 'I Gave My Love a Diamond' a Ben E. King possessed by a demon of cuban-heel angst. 'Turn On Your Lovelight' even sees him emulating the trademark squall of Bobby 'Blue' Bland. Like Mick Jagger or Eric Burdon he synthesizes his R&B and soul influences into a delinquent vocal attitude; unlike them he is a genuinely great singer, with a raw resonance and a nervy, breathless phrasing that verges at moments on psychosis.

The Van Morrison of Them made the ugly, the uncouth, sound beautiful. In much the same way as Hank Williams, whose records he heard in his father's collection as a young boy, he attacks words, seizing and spewing them out until he's exorcized the self-disgust that generates them. Listen to the version of Paul Simon's doomy folk ballad 'Richard Cory' and hear the voice twist and turn, slurring and swallowing phrases with an almost regurgitative violence.

It was Bert Berns, the New York producer flown over to London by Decca to produce Them, who realized how great Morrison was. Berns, too, who sent Van a one-way ticket to the Big Apple when Them finally disintegrated through bloody-mindedness. The story goes that Berns even offered Morrison the chance to collaborate on 'Piece Of My Heart', a song which subsequently became a hit for Aretha Franklin's sister Erma and for Janis Joplin's Big Brother and the Holding Company. Aside from the charming 'Brown-Eyed Girl', an American top ten hit which not only drew on the Latin feel of Bert Berns's earlier productions for Atlantic but anticipated Morrison songs like 'Domino', 'Wild Night', and 'Bulbs', Van's records for Berns's Bang label were oddly unsatisfactory: long, rambling songs like

'He Ain't Give You None' and the grotesque 'T.B. Sheets', together with the insipid originals of 'Beside You' and 'Madame George'. As a midway point between the Morrison of 'Richard Cory' and the Morrison of *Astral Weeks*, they completely lacked the arrangements and dynamics that inspire great vocal performances.

Astral Weeks, recorded in two eight-hour sessions in 1968 and released at the end of that year, really is the masterpiece everybody says it is. With its revolutionary jazz-folk instrumentation and Larry Fallon string arrangements, the album gives Morrison's voice a freedom and scope it had never before enjoyed, and which it has never really enjoyed since: a platform for vocal play and improvisation unrivalled in the history of pop music. Its magnificence has nothing to do with Van's metamorphosis from Angry Young Man into gypsy troubadour. As Johnny Rogan rightly makes clear in his 1984 book on Morrison, the myth of Van the Man as mystical seer is so much Celtic baloney, serving only to obscure what makes this landmark LP so extraordinary, which is simply the sound of a voice going to the end of its tether in pursuit of something that will always elude it. Ralph J. Gleason, after the Irish tenor John McCormack, called it 'the yarrrrragh in the voice'; Lester Bangs called it 'the Revealed Word', adding that Morrison is always 'waiting for a vision to unfold, trying as unobtrusively as possible to nudge it along'.

Whatever it is, it's clear that on *Astral Weeks*, and especially on 'Cyprus Avenue', 'Madame George', and 'Ballerina', Van Morrison gets closer to exposing the naked cry at the heart of human singing than anyone has ever done. In these performances, 'meaning' becomes irrelevant as the voice wrings all sense out of words, scrapes out their innards and tears out their lining. What Bangs called Van's 'whole set of verbal tics' is really a primal subversion of meaning, an attempt to outstrip language through incantation and repetition, the goal being *jouissance*, an ecstatic dissolution of self. This is the 'inarticulate speech of the heart'. 'My t-t-tongue gets t-t-tied, every every t-time I t-try to speak', he stutters in 'Cyprus Avenue'; 'I'm standing in your doorway and I'm mumbling and I can't remember the last thing that ran through my head', he cries in 'Ballerina'. Sense is useless, blocked: what matters is the 'grain' of the wailing tenor voice as it flows and floats out of him, the gibbering, dizzying melisma of 'the writing's on the wall' in 'Ballerina', the tongue rolling around the mouth, the black sound ringing through the nose. There is no straining here, no pushing. As Greil Marcus wrote of *Saint Dominic's Preview*'s 'Listen To The Lion', 'He sings, chants, moans, cries, pleads, shouts, hollers, whispers, until finally he breaks away from language and speaks in Irish tongues, breaking away from ordinary meaning until he has loosed the lion inside himself . . . he is not singing it, it is singing him.' To feel that you are *being sung*: this is the vision, then, the 'yarrrrragh'. No wonder Van Morrison has had to seek shelter in one religion after another ever since. Few singers have tried to lose themselves, to touch God through abandonment, quite so transparently.

Morrison never sang again as he sang on *Astral Weeks*. (On-stage, his frustration, even terror, at not being able to lose himself sometimes made the whole act of performance unbearable.) For all the fleeting thrills – the breathtaking cries in 'Into the Mystic' and 'Brand New Day', the beautiful falsetto performances of 'Crazy Love', 'Gypsy Queen', and 'Who Was That Masked Man?', the bravura celebrations of soul and R&B on the live *It's Too Late to Stop Now* – the voice has steadily deteriorated over the years to the point where it now sounds irreparably clogged and congested. As though giving himself up to his self-loathing, even while singing of redemption, he has become ever more sloppy and grouchy, at times verging on a Dylan-esque disdain for melodic niceties: strange for someone still lauded as a great singer by the Wet Wet Wets of this world. Since switching from Warner Brothers to Phonogram in 1979, he has tended to sing as though his mouth is full of molasses, and his short-winded, grumpily lazy delivery makes one think of Gertrude's description of Hamlet: 'he's fat and scant of breath'. Give me the bolshy punk of 'Gloria' over the bloated bard of *A Sense of Wonder* or *No Guru, No Method, No Teacher* any day.

A singer who came out of the same folk-jazz axis as *Astral Weeks* and chased the same moment of vocal abandon as Morrison was Tim Buckley, that wayward and tormented Californian who died from a heroin overdose in the summer of 1975. (He even recorded a song called 'Gypsy Woman', to go with all those gypsy songs by Van.) His voice, which could stretch from high baritone through piercing countertenor to yelping falsetto, was a crazed instrument, a jazz voice gone mad with its sense of possibility – perhaps not surprising for someone who'd learned to sing as a boy listening to high trumpet notes and low baritone saxophones. Like Van Morrison, he heard Hank Williams at an early age, and fell so deeply in love with country music that he taught himself the banjo.

The first two albums for Elektra, *Tim Buckley* (1966) and *Goodbye And Hello* (1967), give scant indication of the radical vocal experimentation to come. Lee Underwood, who played guitar for Tim for several years, wrote in a long *down beat* piece that he'd watched the singer 'grow from a Bambi-eyed littleboy poet prattling about paper hearts and Valentines' into, successively, 'a hurricane-haired rock'n'roller', 'a madman/genius improvisational vocalist', and 'a lowdown, roadhouse, sex-thumping stomper who injected steam and blood and juice into an R&B music nobody cared about'. I defy anyone to make a coherent connection between 'Once I Was' (1967), 'Starsailor' (1970), and 'Wanda Lou' (1974): the first, from *Goodbye and Hello*, is a wimpish, hopelessly dated piece of folk-rock poesy, sung by a wandering, curly-haired minstrel in a voice as artfully artless as Art Garfunkel's; the second, the title track of the boldest Buckley record of all, is a freeform, multi-tracked maelstrom of overlapping wails, howls, and groans rivalled only by Diamanda Galas's *Litanies of Satan*; and the third, from *Look at the Fool*, is a sassy, 'Louie, Louie'-derived blast of '70s rock'n'soul, belted out like Robert Palmer. The boy certainly covered a lot of bases.

You can just hear the real Tim Buckley coming through on *Goodbye and Hello*'s 'I Never Asked to Be Your Mountain': a cracked, ranting falsetto bringing the song to its incantatory climax. But it's on the third album *Happy/Sad* (1968), recorded after a period of saturation in Coltrane and Coleman, in Miles and Monk and Mingus, that his strange, almost inverted version of the jazz voice fully emerges, complete with a low-key backdrop of acoustic bass, vibes, and marimba. (The live *Dream Letter* album, recorded in 1968 in London and released twenty-two years later, should also be heard in this connection.) 'He was learning how to select words not only for their content,' wrote Lee Underwood, 'but for their round, harsh, or voluptuous sounds.' 'My business is sound,' said Buckley, and in these long, dreamlike pieces – 'Strange Feelin'', based on Miles's 'All Blues', was 7.49 minutes long, while 'Gypsy Woman' clocked in at 12.19 – he begins to play with sound, alternating between clean tone and distortion, *bel canto* purity and open-throat abrasiveness. One minute he's gliding by like Mel Tormé (the 'velvet fog'), the next shrieking like a tomcat; now heaving into a phrase like a black contralto, now swooping up like an impassioned Streisand.

Things got much further out on *Lorca* (1969) and *Starsailor* (1970), albums which for the most part forsook any kind of formal rock structure. Not only were the songs – if songs you could call them – in strange time-signatures like 5/4 and 10/4, but the voice had moved that much closer to pure instrumental sound, free of semantic reference. Introduced by Lee Underwood to the avant-garde singer Cathy Berberian, who 'clucked, gurgled, sighed, yowled, spluttered, screamed, cried, wept, and wailed' on songs by Luciano Berio, Buckley in turn began experimenting with what ambivalent critics called 'vocal gymnastics', luxuriating in the pure modulation of texture and wreaking havoc with melody. On 'Monterey', for example, there are shrieks, bleats, yodels, ululations, and a high cry that could almost be a Miles Davis trumpet note. 'The most shocking thing I've ever seen people come up against is dealing with someone who doesn't sing words,' he said. 'If I had my way, words wouldn't mean a thing.' More self-consciously than Van Morrison, Buckley seemed intent on pushing vocal sound beyond the human voice, and if the resulting dissonance and atonality cost him the love of the Love generation (who only wanted to hear 'Buzzin' Fly' and 'Morning Glory'), he at least felt some kinship with his jazz and avant-garde heroes. *Starsailor* was as radical as a major-label 'rock artist' ever got.

A two-year descent into drugs and alcoholism followed the album's almost total commercial failure, and when he finally made it back there was no way round compromise. Tim Buckley Mark 3, the voice of *Greetings from LA*, *Sefronia*, and *Look at the Fool*, was a bohemian sex machine, a white Al Green who managed to work his insatiable vocal rage into a new and comparatively conventional rock-funk format, whether scatting through the lewd 'Get On Top' or breezing balladeer-style through the superb soul of 'Sweet Surrender', 'Because of You', and 'Look at the Fool'. If the material seemed restrictive, he sounded like he was enjoying himself more than ever: recorded live on a bootleg from LA's Starwood Theatre shortly before his death, he whoops it up like Elvis Presley, Iggy Pop, and Janis Joplin rolled into one. This is what Tim Buckley called his 'monkey-rub, belly-to-belly' voodoo sex music, and he never sounded better than when he was singing it.

A very different product of LA's rock'n'roll underbelly, but a singer as magnificent in his way as Buckley or Morrison, is Michael McDonald, a self-effacing boy from St Louis who headed west to make it as a songwriter only to find himself in 1976 fronting that archetypal southern California band the Doobie Brothers when lead singer Tom Johnston's bad health forced him to quit. McDonald always looked out of place in the Doobies – his dumpy physique and square image were never quite right next to the long hair and shades of the original members – and his singer–songwriter sensibility had even less to do with the sound of *The Captain and Me*. But it was his AOR soul voice, fresh from backing vocal duties with the likes of Steely Dan, which gave the band a new lease of life in the late '70s, and his songs which gave them some of the biggest hits of their career.

On first hearing – probably the Doobies' 1979 No. 1 'What a Fool Believes' – the voice might have sounded a bit sun-bleached, a bit fuzzily anodyne. One was hearing it, after all, through ears numbed by punk and new wave and processing it through a prejudice against all things Californian. By the time *Michael McDonald* appeared in 1982, the richness and pathos of this voice were rather more apparent, and the Top 5 hit 'I Keep Forgettin'' (based loosely on the Leiber & Stoller song Chuck Jackson recorded in the early '60s) opened more minds to its seamless phrasing and rich, aching timbre. Eight years later, despite releasing only two other albums in the intervening eight years, he is a veritable 'singers' singer', with a huge cult following among musos the world over and jazz-funk fans all the way from Romford to Great Yarmouth.

Unless it's a black version of Don Henley, Michael McDonald doesn't sound like anyone else. The voice veers from a breathy intimacy in which you literally feel the air passing up his throat to a yearning tenor-cum-falsetto cry that leaves your hair standing on end. From songs like 'You Belong to Me' and 'There's a Light', essentially solo performances within the framework of Doobies albums, to magical '80s ballads like 'Our Love' and the Burt Bacharach-produced duet with Patti Labelle 'On My Own', his vocal instincts have been unerring. He loves consonants, which is what gives his enunciation such poignant directness and what saves the voice from a glib 'soulfulness'. Every word is placed with a quiet deliberation – listen to 'cost' in 'On My Own', or 'care' and 'cling' in 'I Can Let Go Now' – and carried with a haunting tremor. He loves vowels, too, and every shape he makes seems to curl and wind round the inimitably jazz-inflected chords of his songs.

'I feel shy about accepting the term "soul singer",' McDonald once told me. 'I think I'm a good singer, but sometimes when I get up there with naturally brilliant black singers it's pretty humbling.' If he's not especially agile or melismatic, however – compare him to sparring partner James Ingram on the Quincy Jones-produced 'Yah Mo B There' – the 'grain' of his voice, with its wise weariness, its qualities of humility and vulnerability, is worth a dozen virtuoso session singers of the Ingram ilk.

Three white Soul Men, then, each of whom has absorbed a multitude of influences from black singers and fashioned them into a voice of painful beauty. Van Morrison, who never recovered from 'the agony in the garden' of *Astral Weeks*; Tim Buckley, who died after three albums of feverishly horny R&B; and Michael McDonald, who – out of the three of them – has learned to let go now.

XI

Holy Fools

THE GREAT JAMAICAN SOUL MEN

Whilst I am no world authority on the Jamaican music known variously over the past three decades as ska, rock steady, and reggae, I do know there are Jamaican voices which thrill and entrance me, and that most of them seem to exist in some kind of relationship with black American soul. In fact, perpetually suspended between Africa and America, Jamaican singers have assimilated soul into a vocal style that is essentially what whites would call 'primitive', adapting the influences of people like Curtis Mayfield to a tradition based in African retentions and hymns from Rastafarian 'grounation' ceremonies.

If the basic ska/reggae rhythm came partly out of a Jamaican attempt to emulate the New Orleans R&B sound of the late '50s, the ethereal, eerily beautiful harmonies of the great Jamaican vocal groups came almost directly from the influence of one American soul act: the Impressions, whose warbling, ice-cool voices can be heard in every trio from the early Wailers to the Mighty Diamonds. Exactly why it was Mayfield's restrained, unearthly voice that made such an impact on the island's music is debatable: a certain serenity, perhaps, a philosophical detachment coupled with an unflinching social message. Suffice to say that his songs were covered by the Wailers ('Keep On Moving'), Burning Spear ('People Get Ready'), Pat Kelly ('You Don't Care'), and many others, and that the fluting falsetto which is so vital an ingredient in the Jamaican trio sound to this day derives in large measure from him.

Soul harmonies held a particular fascination for Joe Higgs, who adapted American songs as one half of the duo Higgs & Wilson and became a mentor to acts like Alton Ellis, the Wailers, and the Wailing Souls. Ellis, juggling Jamaican rhythm with an American vocal sensibility in the mid-'60s heyday of the 'rock steady' sound, once said he was 'capable of placing a song *so properly* within rock steady rhythm that you could *hear* the R&B flavour and *feel* the rock steady rhythm at the same time'. It was a statement that many of his fellow singers could have made, even after reggae had undergone its great Rasta revolution at the end of the '60s. For if the 'wailing' voices of this new sound, with their modal harmonies and devotional, chant-like drone, were symptomatic of the 'Back To Africa' sensibility, many of the individual voices only too clearly betrayed their American influences. For every trio like the Ethiopians or the Abyssinians, there was a voice like Toots Hibbert's or Slim Smith's.

Slim Smith's voice was a strange variation on Curtis Mayfield's. Cool and clean, shorn of assertive or demonstrative emotion, it had a deadpan beauty and sliding melisma that combined the restraint of a Johnny Ace with the 'play' of a Sam Cooke, incorporating a kind of 'woah-oh-oh' yodel into his haunting, non-committal delivery. Among the soul songs Smith cut were Eddie Floyd's 'Don't Tell Your Mama', on which he was a dead ringer for Smokey Robinson, and Billy Stewart's 'Sitting in the Park', a Chicago uptown classic that fell squarely into the Curtis Mayfield bag. Toots's sound was distinctly more southern, uncannily close to the frayed baritone timbre of Otis Redding, though there was something too of the Al Green of 'Love Ritual' in there, and of Ray Charles by way of Joe Cocker. Appropriately he cut Otis's 'I've Got Dreams to Remember' on his '80s soul album *Toots in Memphis*, and was joined on the LP by another great Redding soundalike, Eddie Hinton.

Bob Marley was never a great singer, starting life by his own admission as 'a skinny kid with a squeaky voice', but he made up for the lack of naturally beautiful tone with his righteous and urgent delivery. Until 1974, too, he had Bunny Wailer's high tenor-cum-falsetto and Peter Tosh's lugubrious baritone to play against, and the three of them were archetypal Impressions disciples. Bunny's in particular is the voice which makes early Wailers classics like 'Small Axe' and 'Duppy Conqueror' the records they are, harmonizing around Marley's strained lead like a gospel falsetto, and on his solo records after departing the group he sounds like a superior version of Marley, investing versions of his friend's songs – from a delightful 'Mellow Mood' to an achingly naked 'Redemption Song' – with a soulful and melodic beauty their originals only hinted at.

Exactly why trios were so predominant in Jamaica may have something to do with the mystical power of the number three, the power of the trinity, but the consensus seems to be that anything larger than a trio made the sound 'too full'. The great harmony groups of reggae thrived above all on space, flexibility, even a kind of ascetic bleakness, and too many voices spoilt the broth. 'Droning doo-wop with a hair-raising edge', Randall Grass called it, and you feel the space between the carefree, insouciant tenors and the leathery, coarsely nasal baritones of these neo-street corner combos, from the Gaylads in the early '60s through the Heptones and the Paragons in reggae's heyday to trios like the Morwells and the Itals in the late '70s. Really they were like a distorting mirror-image of American vocal groups: even with sweet, smooth voices like those of Leroy Sibbles in the Heptones and John Holt in the Paragons, they managed to subvert the creamy, dreamy harmonies of soul with a marvellous rawness. If the militant Mighty Diamonds covered songs by the Stylistics, and the militant Meditations were still studying Impressions records in 1980, the results remained the same: a wailing, trancelike, elemental soul music which warped and twisted American soul's harmonies and call-and-response patterns to superbly unpredictable ends.

The ultimate 'roots' trio was Burning Spear, whose possessed, shaman-like frontman Spear (Winston Rodney) had a soul voice of incomparable power and beauty and whose harmony singers Rupert Willington and Delroy Hines provided grimly devotional backing – 'a Greek chorus out of African griot tradition', in Randall Grass's words. Spear is the Holy Fool *par excellence*, a singer whose every keening, burnished phrase seems to be sung by something outside him, and who sounds simultaneously enraptured and hysterical with grief. On Studio One recordings of the late '60s he is admirably restrained, with a pure, beautifully concentrated tone and a gingerly kind of enunciation in which he barely hits hard consonants while leaning heavily on the patois of his vowels. The timing is spine-tingling, with never a breath out of place and with words draped effortlessly across the crude step of the rhythm. One senses the immense power he is holding back, a searing passion which only rears up in the sudden cries he looses out of nowhere on songs like the mighty 'Door Peeper'. This is the mad and harsh sobbing we come to expect by the time of *Marcus Garvey* (1975) – our cathartic reward and release.

The Spear of the great Island albums is simply awesome. Rodney is as obsessive and crazed a vocal artist as any of the great singers *qua* singers I have considered so far in *From a Whisper to a Scream*. Feel the pleasure he takes in the shapes of his words: 'travelling' becoming 'truvlane', 'slavery' osmosing into 'slayvreh', 'more than two thousand miles' transmuted into 'moredantootouzanmile', with each vowel stretched out on a rack of harsh nasality. Feel him drop phrases into the rhythmic flow like pearls, always a crucial split-second behind – on the tail of – the beat. Feel the quick draw of breath before each phrase, the little soul quiver at the end, the complete immersion in a song's movement as he flows within its every warp and woof. There is nothing else in reggae like the preacher's cry of 'Throw Down Your Arms', of the thunderous 'Civilized Reggae', of 'Jah no dead/Jah no dead/Jah no dead/Jah no dead/Jah no dead' in 'Marcus Say Jah No Dead', and there probably never will be.

Another extraordinary singer, whose freakishly beautiful falsetto makes him worthy of comparison with the likes of Aaron Neville, is Horace Andy. Distinctive is not the word for this disarmingly girlish sound, with its inconsolable Little Anthony timbre and orgasmically shuddered vibrato: the man is a true original. 'She says I'm just a little boy', he sings on the Studio One-recorded 'Love of a Woman', and he still sounds like a little boy on menacing '80s records like 'Fight Fight' and 'Curfew'. For this is a child playing adult lover, an archangel following in the mortal footsteps of Studio One peers like Slim Smith and Ken Boothe, and the effect is nothing short of bizarre. When Horace emits one of his convulsive squeals, pinching vowels into a highly ambiguous kind of pain, it's as though the sound is being tickled out of him, and one can only shiver in response.

The late '70s and '80s were dominated by solo singers like Andy – and by DJs who turned the reggae voice into something which went way beyond mere singing. Of the singers, Gregory Isaacs presented a new kind of Jamaican Soul Man image, all three-piece suits and loose-limbed vulnerability, and sang in a cool, sleepily seductive tenor that made him something of a heart-throb both at home and abroad. 'He constructs melodic lines from a monotonal African scale in which he feels most comfortable,' wrote Stephen Davis, and the effect, together with a forlorn kind of phrasing reminiscent of Slim Smith, was often mesmerizing, if ultimately a little *too* comfortable. A less limited, less one-dimensional voice was that of Dennis Brown, whose breathy, high-spirited tenor seemed to dance through songs with a dreamy, wavering vibrato. Half the pleasure of this fruity, resonant sound was in his chewed, burbled delivery, which created its own haphazard music.

Freddie McGregor sounds like a cross between Dennis Brown and Tyrone Davis, which is about as 'soulful' as reggae gets. Another Impressions junkie during his early days with the Clarendonians, his voice has matured through his Studio One years from a high, fluttering tenor into a gorgeous, richly resonant instrument that can do as much justice to a soul song like Ronnie Dyson's 'Just Don't Want to Be Lonely' as could Tyrone Davis himself. In comparison, voices like those of Barrington Levy and Frankie Paul seem crude and graceless, though Levy has a lean, lithe tone and a delirious patois playfulness to his credit.

✳

The reggae voice is the wailer's voice: the voice, in Wailing Soul 'Bread' MacDonald's words, of 'a soul crying in the wilderness'. And if one hears this cry through the strafing of Kingston gunfire, or through a cloud of ganja-fuelled 'spirituality', that does not make it any the less pure or wild.

XII

A New King and Queen

LUTHER VANDROSS AND ANITA BAKER

When Luther Vandross emerged from the tail-end of the disco age in the early '80s, it was as a survivor of a bleak phase in the annals of soul singing. Indeed, despite an association with the David Bowie of *Young Americans* that led to two '70s albums by his group Luther, Vandross only really began to be noticed around the turn of the decade as an anonymous session voice on jingles and on sides by a cut-price version of Chic called Change. Disco had all but killed off the soul voice defined in the '60s, and most of the great Soul Men I've written about in this book were, in no uncertain terms, out in the cold.

Vandross's big 1981 hit 'Never Too Much' signalled the coming of a new kind of Soul Man, and one which dominated the ensuing decade. This was the Ladykiller, the big, bejewelled teddy bear promising security and respect, roses and candlelight – and delivering a voice that would melt the inhibitions of the coldest love-object. By 1985 ballads were back in, and Freddie Jackson could opine that they 'put you in the circuit for longevity as a performer'. The voice was once again a virtuoso instrument, not simply a vehicle for a 12″ dance mix.

That Vandross was not only the first but far and away the greatest of these Soul Men now seems self-evident. As a singer, songwriter, arranger, and producer, he has been in a class of his own for almost ten years, making records of astonishing beauty and inventiveness and honing his art to near-perfection. His experience as a backing singer and 'vocal contractor' in the heady session world of New York has served him in invaluable stead, giving him both the humility and the discipline to build a long-term career he was initially wary of pursuing. He still uses the same gaggle of friends he sang with through his leaner years, and their shimmering, supernatural harmonies on his records bear eloquent testimony to his long apprenticeship as an arranger. (After working with Bowie he did backing vocals for Bette Midler, Carly Simon, and Quincy Jones, and arranged all the vocal parts on the Barbra Streisand/Donna Summer duet 'Enough is Enough'.)

As a solo singer and songwriter, his work betrays his adolescent immersion in uptown pop-soul from Burt Bacharach to Tamla Motown, in records which – like vocal harmonies – he never simply listened to but actively *studied*. Ironically, this ladykiller's vocal models are all women, particularly the big three of Dionne Warwick, Aretha Franklin, and Diana Ross. In contrast to the likes of Alexander O'Neal, and in extreme contrast to ladykilling forebears like the gruff-voiced Teddy Pendergrass, Vandross's Soul Man aesthetic has precious little to do with sweaty sexuality. 'People tend to see me platonically, fraternally,' he says. 'They don't lust.' The voice itself bears this out: Luther's singing is not about passion or libido as such, but about grace and beauty, control and restraint, finesse and craftsmanship. There is something almost effeminate in his meticulous attention to detail, and the voice, building from a dark, glossy baritone to a breathily intimate falsetto, often sounds more like a camp composite of his favourite divas than like, say, Marvin Gaye. This is why he feels so comfortable with the ritzy, bravura balladry of Bacharach's great Dionne Warwick vehicles, 'A House Is Not a Home', 'Anyone Who Had a Heart'. Luther Vandross, a cabaret earth mama? It's not so far from the truth.

He tends to dismiss his early recordings as the work of a singer prone to the classic crime of 'oversouling', clobbering the listener over the head instead of seducing him. 'You're trying to prove something when you're young, and now I have nothing to prove.' Actually, the voice of his two Cotillion albums is all but fully formed, as 'This Close To You' and the original version of *Any Love*'s 'The Second Time Around' amply demonstrate. It's a big, rounded voice with a thick, rich timbre – a tenor that resonates like a baritone, one might almost call it – but he uses it with a jazz singer's precision and inflections. His staple trick is to pass in and out of falsetto, permanently hovering between the chest and head voices, and the effect is that of a picture repeatedly coming in and out of focus. Individual words are accented within the warm flow of his vocal lines as the voice caresses, then pulls away from, the mike. Simultaneously, he is one moment racing ahead of the beat and the next lagging behind it. Overall, he exhibits an extraordinary kind of control, a relationship with the song that is all about delaying gratification, deferring the moment of catharsis.

The voice comes properly into its own on the *Never Too Much* album: on the long, undulating lines of the up-tempo title track; on 'A House Is Not a Home', first of his epic LP finales; and on the gorgeous 'You Stopped Loving Me', a song that blueprinted a certain kind of mid-tempo style for Vandross. The performance of the Bacharach song is as definitive as Sinatra's interpretation of, say, 'My Funny Valentine', a seven-minute *tour de force* of polished, pared-down sensuality that's become a *de rigueur* showstopper at his live appearances. The vibrato is contained but swirling, multi-hued, and if there is a slight sense of 'showiness' in the phrasing it is always offset by tiny cracks and tears in the legato flow. In the latter half of the song he builds towards his climax with mantra-like repetitions – 'Are you gonna be, say you're gonna be, are you gonna be/Still in love, still in love . . .' – setting precedents for all his subsequent 'epics': 'Superstar', 'The Other Side of the World', 'Anyone Who Had a Heart', 'Love Won't Let Me Wait', and 'The Second Time Around'. On 'You Stopped Loving Me' he demonstrates the kind of telepathic chemistry with his backing singers that Aretha Franklin enjoyed with the Sweet Inspirations: no surprise that ex-Sweet Inspiration Cissy Houston, mother of Whitney, has been an integral part of Luther's vocal team from the beginning.

With each album Vandross has become stronger, subtler. In bassist Marcus Miller he has found a co-writer/producer of near-genius, and together they have fashioned a techno-soul sound which combines the very best of the old and the new, the raw and the cooked, and which serves rather than detracts from the refined emotion of his voice. On 'The Night I Fell In Love' and 'See Me', the voice floats serenely around Yogi Horton's hypnotic drum programmes; on 'The Other Side of the World', a vocal recorded in one take at four in the morning, glides through an almost ambient soundscape. ('My favourite time in the studio is in the middle of the night, no lights at all, no one around except the engineer and Marcus in the other room sleeping. The escape is unreal. I'm impenetrable and vulnerable to nothing at that point and it's the best . . .') Whether it's on the slap-bass pop-funk of 'I Wanted Your Love' and "Til My Baby Comes Home', the schmaltzy balladry of 'If Only for One Night' and 'There's Nothing Better Than Love', or the hi-tech rock'n'soul of 'Stop to Love' and 'Give Me the Reason', Luther's singing is fluid, acrobatic, weightless.

Onstage the weightlessness of the voice, conducting what Vandross calls his 'musical séance', more than compensates for the lack of physical agility that has hacks still calling him 'the Pavarotti of Pop'. When I saw him in 1989 in the small and comparatively intimate Circle Star near San Francisco, he looked like an improbable cross between Solomon Burke, that portly bishop of soul, and Sylvester, the late, lovable disco queen. With him on the small circular stage were his exotic singer-dancers Lisa Fisher, Kevin Owens, and *Young Americans* veteran Ava Cherry, figures who offset and choreographed emotions which he himself couldn't enact. Padding about like some camp banana republic dictator, he was an awkward, unco-ordinated figure amidst the other graceful forms, but then all his energy and concentration were dedicated to one thing, which was lifting his notes into the audience and filling the theatre with the ache of their sound. And inevitably the black matrons with their plastic roses cried out softly 'Sing it, baby', 'Take your time', urging him to hold back on 'A House Is Not a Home' as though he were making passionate love to each one of them. 'Sometimes when I'm onstage I think about being lonely,' he said to me after the show. 'Sometimes I get so, so, so, so fuckin' depressed that I just close my eyes and almost dissociate myself from the planet . . . because I'm not singing ditties here, these are not little lightweight songs. These are songs which call upon things that have happened to you – or more important, that *haven't* happened to you.'

'What a world for the lonely kind', he sang on the title track of *Any Love* (1988), and the song was as private and emotional as Vandross has ever got. Like the Sinatra of *Only the Lonely*, like most of the singers in this book, he turns his hurt into art and redeems it in the process. On 'Any Love' and 'For You to Love', perhaps the two most perfect songs he and Marcus Miller have written to date, his fragile, almost tentative lead is cushioned by his own background vocals, a lonely cry resonating in a solipsistic hall of mirrors. On 'Love Won't Let Me Wait', he turns Major Harris's lewd 1974 classic into a devotional, quasi-religious epic about union with the beloved wherein every last orgasmic shudder, every 'I'm coming, I'm coming', is irreproachably tasteful and touching.

Whether or not Vandross can top the miraculous *Any Love* in the '90s, he has – like Luciano Pavarotti, indeed – remarkably little competition. Of the other ladykillers to emerge in the second half of the '80s, only Alexander O'Neal has as special a voice, higher and considerably more nasal than Luther's but equally beautiful. His trembling vibrato and wonderfully open vowels almost connect him with the sobbing tradition of Clyde McPhatter and Jackie Wilson, while his wistful sighs and deft juggling of machismo and vulnerability make him the Gregory Isaacs of soul: 'If You Were Here Tonight' is his 'Night Nurse'. Certainly it's a more affecting voice than that of Freddie Jackson, whose ornate, ultra-mannered melisma, tumbling and swirling over endless permutations of Marvin Gaye's 'Sexual Healing', is really a rococo perversion of the Vandross voice. This Gucci seducer is like a dancer or a gymnast trying to cram as many tricks into as short a space of time as possible: he can't let a phrase go by without stamping it with virtuoso overkill. David Peaston, hailed as the 'new Vandross' in 1989, is rather the same, showering his material with rampant, gratuitous melisma as if taking part in some Olympics of singing. This is the ultimate

fetishization of the gospel voice, and even on the rather pretentious treatment of Billie Holiday's 'God Bless the Child' Peaston's high tenor-cum-shrieking falsetto sounds like a cross
between Freddie Jackson and gospel singer Rance Allen. In the
baritone range, meanwhile, the deep, breezily resonant voice of
Will Downing sounded fabulous on the Arthur Baker-produced
'A Love Supreme', and still sounds great if slightly sub-Luther-
esque on the jazz ballad 'Too Soon' (1989), but he lacks the
rich virility of a Jeffrey Osborne – as well as Vandross's imagination.

It's appropriate that when Luther Vandross began the American leg of his 1988 World Tour he shared the bill with Anita
Baker, his only female equivalent as a contemporary soul singer.
Together they were the King and Queen of the Quiet Storm, of
sophisticated 'fireside' soul music, and together they crossed the
States filling gigantic arenas with aspiring buppies. Only when
Luther made the apparently presumptuous request that they
record a duet together did the royal marriage – made in soul
heaven – break down. 'Don't even ask,' was Baker's terse reply.

Anita Baker is a pretty affable and good-natured gal, which
makes that story all the more surprising. But perhaps it says
something about the distance she perceives between her music
and the rest of the soul mainstream. For although her songs fall
loosely into the 'fireside' soul ballad bag, she is a very different
proposition to the myriad other soulstresses – characterless,
interchangeable – out there. Not only is she tiny, quite plain,
and decidedly unglamorous, but she has a voice that has nothing
to do with the tedious, ultra-coded conventions of today's soul
singing and dance music. Influenced as much by Sarah Vaughan
and Nancy Wilson as by the music she heard in her local Baptist
and Pentecostal churches, she sings soul like a jazz singer, with
jazz intelligence, jazz fluidity, and jazz mannerisms. In fact, the

whole mode of her singing, her articulation and 'expression', is that of an instrument, half alto saxophone, perhaps, and half trumpet, and she plays the instrument with the same controlled abandon as any great jazzman.

Nelson George dubbed Baker's style 'retronuevo', defined as 'an embracing of the past to create passionate, fresh expressions and institutions'. But there is nothing contrived or nostalgic about this particular embrace, just as her voice is never studiedly 'jazzy'. From *The Songstress* (1983) through to the disappointing *Compositions* (1990), she has combined dazzling technique with a plaintive edge worthy of Michael McDonald (her 'baby' is pure McDonald). The first album showed her phenomenal range, from a smoky, artful alto to an untrammelled soprano that fleetingly suggested Stephanie Mills, but it was the rapturous *Rapture* (1986) that showed her elasticity, her tendency to climb from line to line and push herself ever higher, like water seeping up to find new levels and fill every available space. Her timbre is pure and smooth, and when unshaded by her very idiosyncratic phrasing, with all its slurs and dips, is almost Caucasian. Similarly, her diction is extremely proper: *poised*, one might say. Finally, she clamps her vowels so tightly that one feels only a steady stream of shapes folding into each other, gliding and sliding through songs as though entranced and magnetized by something outside itself. 'You become a vessel,' she says of her singing. 'It's like having an out-of-body experience.' In the unique, unfurling trajectories of her vocal lines there is above all the unaffected joy of vocal exploration, and the little scat passages on the magnificent 'Been So Long' were hardly a surprise. By *Giving You the Best That I Got* (1988), she was assured enough to attempt the straight jazz of 'Good Enough', and to bring it off with flying colours. 'Giving You the Best' itself was the greatest thing she's ever done, a sinuously spare, dreamily relaxed ballad with plenty of space for each perfectly apportioned phrase that floated out of her birdlike frame.

As with Vandross, no one else can really touch Baker. There was some fuss about Regina Belle back in 1987, but when it came down to it, despite doing a very good Billie Holiday take on 'So Many Tears', she turned out to be nothing more than proficient. Aretha and Randy Crawford are still singing, but Anita Baker is way out on her own as a vocal artist of genius.

AFTERWORD

'Isn't it the truth of the voice to be hallucinated?', asked Roland Barthes, and to a great extent the principal voices of this book have been, and continue to be, hallucinatory presences in my life, shadows of beings whose precise nature it is maddeningly difficult to locate. 'We know since Pythagoras that music can heal,' wrote George Steiner in *Heidegger*, 'and since Plato that there are in music agencies which can literally madden . . . But what is it? . . . Where, in the phenomenon "music", do we locate the energies which can transmute the fabric of human consciousness in listener and performer?' In attempting to 'describe' my voices – to force language on an art form which has nothing to do with language except insofar as it uses words in its production – I have frequently felt crazed and paralysed, even if much of what I've written has only skirted around the real issue. If Barthes is right that we are bound by 'an imaginary of music criticism whose function it is to *constitute* me as a listener', then how may I break out of that critical trap?

Nietzsche wrote that 'it is only through the spirit of music that we can understand the joy involved in the annihilation of the individual'. But we can't 'understand' it if we persist in trying to describe something that has no meaning for us *as describers* (or should that be de-scriptors?). If music is the irrational undoing of our 'constituted' egos, then we must simply give ourselves up to it, allow ourselves to be swallowed into its healing madness. The problem with hearing *voices* is that they are *apparently* close to us, *apparently* constituted as human and language-bound, in a way that a violin concerto, for example, obviously isn't. As Luciano Berio said, 'From the grossest of noises to the most delicate singing, the voice always means something, always refers beyond itself and creates a huge range of associations: cultural, musical, emotive, physiological, or drawn from everyday life . . .'

And yet, of course, the moment a voice begins to sing, to cry out from the pit of the singer's physical being, it overreaches the bounds of communication. It becomes, as Barthes says, 'a signifying play having nothing to do with communication', perhaps even a message, in Gregory Bateson's words, 'about the interface between conscious and unconscious'. Which means that we can only try to say what voices *do*, how – Barthes again – they 'work at the language'.

Needless to say – and especially since I am hardly a musicologist and can only bluff my way through musical jargon – I have been unable to resist describing voices as 'harrowing', 'plaintive', and so on. In the end one resorts to the inevitable epithet, and I must presume that the power of these sounds – sounds which, however 'human', transcend our framework of emotional reference – is too threatening not to be processed through such humanistic mediation.

While many of the voices in this book have haunted me, resounded in my head like ghosts that will not be placated, so I have myself always sung, and found both relief and intoxication (healing and madness, come to that) in doing so. When I actually took the plunge and started performing and recording as 'a singer' in 1987, I came to understand just how extraordinary the voices of my favourite singers were: how instinctive, how effortless, how unselfconscious. I do not know how often these singers have genuinely 'lost themselves' in the act of singing, how often they've felt that they were 'being sung' and that their voices were somehow outside of themselves, but I do know that the business of singing (let alone of entertaining!) eventually became too premeditated an affair for me to continue pursuing its elusive rewards. And this, I suppose, must have something to do with having written about music for too long, with being 'a critic' who cannot operate with what Simon Reynolds calls 'UNKNOWINGNESS'. Or maybe I just can't sing . . .

'I knew that I had only to sing,' says a character in one of E. T. A. Hoffmann's stories, 'and I should live again in you wholly, for every note was sleeping in your heart.' I imagine that as a singer I was trying to touch off something inside people that all of my favourite voices touch off in me – the 'reasons in the heart', which, as Bateson wrote, 'reason doesn't perceive'.

BIBLIOGRAPHY

The following books and articles were invaluable in the preparation for *From a Whisper to a Scream*:

BOB ALLEN, *George Jones: The Saga of an American Singer* (New York, Doubleday, 1984)

WHITNEY BALLIETT, *American Singers* (New York, OUP, 1988)

LESTER BANGS, 'Astral Weeks' in Greil Marcus (ed.) *Psychotic Reactions and Carburetor Dung* (New York, Knopf, 1987)

KEN BARNES *et al.*, *Sinatra and the Great Song Stylists* (London, Ian Allan, 1972)

ROLAND BARTHES, 'The Grain of the Voice' in *Image-Music-Text* (London, Fontana, 1977)

BRIAN CASE, 'A Flag for Lady Day', *Time Out*, 5–11 July 1984

ALAN DURANT, *Conditions of Music* (London, Macmillan, 1984)

J. B. FIGI, 'Time Out For Bobby Bland', *down beat*, 7 August 1969

GARY GIDDINS, *Riding On a Blue Note* (New York, OUP, 1981)

RANDALL GRASS, 'The Great Jamaican Harmony Trios' in *Reggae International* (London, Thames & Hudson, 1983)

PETER GURALNICK, *Lost Highway* (Boston, David R. Godine, 1979)

ANTHONY HEILBUT, *The Gospel Sound* (New York, Limelight, 1985)

GERRI HIRSHEY, *Nowhere to Run* (New York, Times Books, 1984)

CHARLES KEIL, *Urban Blues* (Chicago, University of Chicago, 1966)

GENE LEES, *Singers and the Song* (New York, OUP, 1987)

KIP LORNELL, *Happy in the Service of the Lord*, (Chicago, University of Illinois, 1988)

MICHAEL LYDON, *Rock Folk* (New York, Delta, 1971)

WILFRED MELLERS, *Angels of the Night: Popular Female Singers of Our Time* (London, Blackwell, 1986)

BILL MILLAR, *The Drifters* (London, Studio Vista, 1971)

JIM MILLER (ed.), *The Rolling Stone Illustrated History of Rock & Roll* (New York, Random House, 1980)

DAVID NATHAN, 'Reflections on Garnet Mimms', *Blues & Soul*, December 1970

PETE NICKOLS, 'The Solomon Burke Story', *Record Collector*, May 1985
'Black Gospel: The Roots of Soul', *Voices From the Shadows*, nos. 2, 3, 4 & 5

JIM O'NEAL and DICK SHURMAN, 'Ted Taylor Interview', *Living Blues*, no. 25, January/February 1976

HENRY PLEASANTS, *The Great American Popular Singers* (New York, Simon & Schuster, 1974)

ROBERT PRUTER, 'The McKinley Mitchell Story', *Juke Blues*, no. 12
'The Mitty Collier Story', *Goldmine*, November 1981
'The Walter Jackson Story', *Soul Survivor*, no. 10

JOHN ROCKWELL, *Sinatra: An American Classic* (New York, Random House, 1984)

JOHNNY ROGAN, *Van Morrison* (London, Proteus, 1984)

PATRICK SNYDER-SCUMPY, 'Etta: The Classic R&B Singer Kicks Back', *Crawdaddy*, November 1974

VAL WILMER, 'Interview with Aretha Franklin', *down beat*, 8 August 1968

INDEX

C

D